C-3012   CAREER EXAMINATION SERIES

*This is your
PASSBOOK for...*

Water Meter Repair Supervisor

*Test Preparation Study Guide
Questions & Answers*

COPYRIGHT NOTICE

This book is SOLELY intended for, is sold ONLY to, and its use is RESTRICTED to individual, bona fide applicants or candidates who qualify by virtue of having seriously filed applications for appropriate license, certificate, professional and/or promotional advancement, higher school matriculation, scholarship, or other legitimate requirements of education and/or governmental authorities.

This book is NOT intended for use, class instruction, tutoring, training, duplication, copying, reprinting, excerption, or adaptation, etc., by:

1) Other publishers
2) Proprietors and/or Instructors of "Coaching" and/or Preparatory Courses
3) Personnel and/or Training Divisions of commercial, industrial, and governmental organizations
4) Schools, colleges, or universities and/or their departments and staffs, including teachers and other personnel
5) Testing Agencies or Bureaus
6) Study groups which seek by the purchase of a single volume to copy and/or duplicate and/or adapt this material for use by the group as a whole without having purchased individual volumes for each of the members of the group
7) Et al.

Such persons would be in violation of appropriate Federal and State statutes.

PROVISION OF LICENSING AGREEMENTS – Recognized educational, commercial, industrial, and governmental institutions and organizations, and others legitimately engaged in educational pursuits, including training, testing, and measurement activities, may address request for a licensing agreement to the copyright owners, who will determine whether, and under what conditions, including fees and charges, the materials in this book may be used them. In other words, a licensing facility exists for the legitimate use of the material in this book on other than an individual basis. However, it is asseverated and affirmed here that the material in this book CANNOT be used without the receipt of the express permission of such a licensing agreement from the Publishers. Inquiries re licensing should be addressed to the company, attention rights and permissions department.

All rights reserved, including the right of reproduction in whole or in part, in any form or by any means, electronic or mechanical, including photocopying, recording, or by any information storage and retrieval system, without permission in writing from the Publisher.

Copyright © 2025 by
National Learning Corporation

212 Michael Drive, Syosset, NY 11791
(516) 921-8888 • www.passbooks.com
E-mail: info@passbooks.com

PASSBOOK® SERIES

THE *PASSBOOK® SERIES* has been created to prepare applicants and candidates for the ultimate academic battlefield – the examination room.

At some time in our lives, each and every one of us may be required to take an examination – for validation, matriculation, admission, qualification, registration, certification, or licensure.

Based on the assumption that every applicant or candidate has met the basic formal educational standards, has taken the required number of courses, and read the necessary texts, the *PASSBOOK® SERIES* furnishes the one special preparation which may assure passing with confidence, instead of failing with insecurity. Examination questions – together with answers – are furnished as the basic vehicle for study so that the mysteries of the examination and its compounding difficulties may be eliminated or diminished by a sure method.

This book is meant to help you pass your examination provided that you qualify and are serious in your objective.

The entire field is reviewed through the huge store of content information which is succinctly presented through a provocative and challenging approach – the question-and-answer method.

A climate of success is established by furnishing the correct answers at the end of each test.

You soon learn to recognize types of questions, forms of questions, and patterns of questioning. You may even begin to anticipate expected outcomes.

You perceive that many questions are repeated or adapted so that you can gain acute insights, which may enable you to score many sure points.

You learn how to confront new questions, or types of questions, and to attack them confidently and work out the correct answers.

You note objectives and emphases, and recognize pitfalls and dangers, so that you may make positive educational adjustments.

Moreover, you are kept fully informed in relation to new concepts, methods, practices, and directions in the field.

You discover that you are actually taking the examination all the time: you are preparing for the examination by "taking" an examination, not by reading extraneous and/or supererogatory textbooks.

In short, this PASSBOOK®, used directedly, should be an important factor in helping you to pass your test.

WATER METER REPAIR SUPERVISOR

DUTIES
The work involves responsibility for the effective and efficient operation, scheduling and supervision of the work activities of the water meter repair and meter reading units of the water department. Does related work as required.

SCOPE OF THE EXAMINATION
The <u>written test</u> will cover knowledge, skills and/or abilities in such areas as:

1. Arithmetic computations;
2. Meter reading;
3. Operation and maintenance of mechanical devices;
4. Use and identification of tools;
5. Operation and servicing of water meters; and
6. Supervision.

HOW TO TAKE A TEST

I. YOU MUST PASS AN EXAMINATION

A. *WHAT EVERY CANDIDATE SHOULD KNOW*

Examination applicants often ask us for help in preparing for the written test. What can I study in advance? What kinds of questions will be asked? How will the test be given? How will the papers be graded?

As an applicant for a civil service examination, you may be wondering about some of these things. Our purpose here is to suggest effective methods of advance study and to describe civil service examinations.

Your chances for success on this examination can be increased if you know how to prepare. Those "pre-examination jitters" can be reduced if you know what to expect. You can even experience an adventure in good citizenship if you know why civil service exams are given.

B. *WHY ARE CIVIL SERVICE EXAMINATIONS GIVEN?*

Civil service examinations are important to you in two ways. As a citizen, you want public jobs filled by employees who know how to do their work. As a job seeker, you want a fair chance to compete for that job on an equal footing with other candidates. The best-known means of accomplishing this two-fold goal is the competitive examination.

Exams are widely publicized throughout the nation. They may be administered for jobs in federal, state, city, municipal, town or village governments or agencies.

Any citizen may apply, with some limitations, such as the age or residence of applicants. Your experience and education may be reviewed to see whether you meet the requirements for the particular examination. When these requirements exist, they are reasonable and applied consistently to all applicants. Thus, a competitive examination may cause you some uneasiness now, but it is your privilege and safeguard.

C. *HOW ARE CIVIL SERVICE EXAMS DEVELOPED?*

Examinations are carefully written by trained technicians who are specialists in the field known as "psychological measurement," in consultation with recognized authorities in the field of work that the test will cover. These experts recommend the subject matter areas or skills to be tested; only those knowledges or skills important to your success on the job are included. The most reliable books and source materials available are used as references. Together, the experts and technicians judge the difficulty level of the questions.

Test technicians know how to phrase questions so that the problem is clearly stated. Their ethics do not permit "trick" or "catch" questions. Questions may have been tried out on sample groups, or subjected to statistical analysis, to determine their usefulness.

Written tests are often used in combination with performance tests, ratings of training and experience, and oral interviews. All of these measures combine to form the best-known means of finding the right person for the right job.

II. HOW TO PASS THE WRITTEN TEST

A. NATURE OF THE EXAMINATION

To prepare intelligently for civil service examinations, you should know how they differ from school examinations you have taken. In school you were assigned certain definite pages to read or subjects to cover. The examination questions were quite detailed and usually emphasized memory. Civil service exams, on the other hand, try to discover your present ability to perform the duties of a position, plus your potentiality to learn these duties. In other words, a civil service exam attempts to predict how successful you will be. Questions cover such a broad area that they cannot be as minute and detailed as school exam questions.

In the public service similar kinds of work, or positions, are grouped together in one "class." This process is known as *position-classification*. All the positions in a class are paid according to the salary range for that class. One class title covers all of these positions, and they are all tested by the same examination.

B. FOUR BASIC STEPS

1) Study the announcement

How, then, can you know what subjects to study? Our best answer is: "Learn as much as possible about the class of positions for which you've applied." The exam will test the knowledge, skills and abilities needed to do the work.

Your most valuable source of information about the position you want is the official exam announcement. This announcement lists the training and experience qualifications. Check these standards and apply only if you come reasonably close to meeting them.

The brief description of the position in the examination announcement offers some clues to the subjects which will be tested. Think about the job itself. Review the duties in your mind. Can you perform them, or are there some in which you are rusty? Fill in the blank spots in your preparation.

Many jurisdictions preview the written test in the exam announcement by including a section called "Knowledge and Abilities Required," "Scope of the Examination," or some similar heading. Here you will find out specifically what fields will be tested.

2) Review your own background

Once you learn in general what the position is all about, and what you need to know to do the work, ask yourself which subjects you already know fairly well and which need improvement. You may wonder whether to concentrate on improving your strong areas or on building some background in your fields of weakness. When the announcement has specified "some knowledge" or "considerable knowledge," or has used adjectives like "beginning principles of..." or "advanced ... methods," you can get a clue as to the number and difficulty of questions to be asked in any given field. More questions, and hence broader coverage, would be included for those subjects which are more important in the work. Now weigh your strengths and weaknesses against the job requirements and prepare accordingly.

3) Determine the level of the position

Another way to tell how intensively you should prepare is to understand the level of the job for which you are applying. Is it the entering level? In other words, is this the position in which beginners in a field of work are hired? Or is it an intermediate or advanced level? Sometimes this is indicated by such words as "Junior" or "Senior" in the class title. Other jurisdictions use Roman numerals to designate the level – Clerk I, Clerk II, for example. The word "Supervisor" sometimes appears in the title. If the level is not indicated by the title, check the description of duties. Will you be working under very close supervision, or will you have responsibility for independent decisions in this work?

4) Choose appropriate study materials

Now that you know the subjects to be examined and the relative amount of each subject to be covered, you can choose suitable study materials. For beginning level jobs, or even advanced ones, if you have a pronounced weakness in some aspect of your training, read a modern, standard textbook in that field. Be sure it is up to date and has general coverage. Such books are normally available at your library, and the librarian will be glad to help you locate one. For entry-level positions, questions of appropriate difficulty are chosen – neither highly advanced questions, nor those too simple. Such questions require careful thought but not advanced training.

If the position for which you are applying is technical or advanced, you will read more advanced, specialized material. If you are already familiar with the basic principles of your field, elementary textbooks would waste your time. Concentrate on advanced textbooks and technical periodicals. Think through the concepts and review difficult problems in your field.

These are all general sources. You can get more ideas on your own initiative, following these leads. For example, training manuals and publications of the government agency which employs workers in your field can be useful, particularly for technical and professional positions. A letter or visit to the government department involved may result in more specific study suggestions, and certainly will provide you with a more definite idea of the exact nature of the position you are seeking.

III. KINDS OF TESTS

Tests are used for purposes other than measuring knowledge and ability to perform specified duties. For some positions, it is equally important to test ability to make adjustments to new situations or to profit from training. In others, basic mental abilities not dependent on information are essential. Questions which test these things may not appear as pertinent to the duties of the position as those which test for knowledge and information. Yet they are often highly important parts of a fair examination. For very general questions, it is almost impossible to help you direct your study efforts. What we can do is to point out some of the more common of these general abilities needed in public service positions and describe some typical questions.

1) General information

Broad, general information has been found useful for predicting job success in some kinds of work. This is tested in a variety of ways, from vocabulary lists to questions about current events. Basic background in some field of work, such as sociology or economics, may be sampled in a group of questions. Often these are principles which have become familiar to most persons through exposure rather than through formal training. It is difficult to advise you how to study for these questions; being alert to the world around you is our best suggestion.

2) Verbal ability

An example of an ability needed in many positions is verbal or language ability. Verbal ability is, in brief, the ability to use and understand words. Vocabulary and grammar tests are typical measures of this ability. Reading comprehension or paragraph interpretation questions are common in many kinds of civil service tests. You are given a paragraph of written material and asked to find its central meaning.

3) Numerical ability

Number skills can be tested by the familiar arithmetic problem, by checking paired lists of numbers to see which are alike and which are different, or by interpreting charts and graphs. In the latter test, a graph may be printed in the test booklet which you are asked to use as the basis for answering questions.

4) Observation

A popular test for law-enforcement positions is the observation test. A picture is shown to you for several minutes, then taken away. Questions about the picture test your ability to observe both details and larger elements.

5) Following directions

In many positions in the public service, the employee must be able to carry out written instructions dependably and accurately. You may be given a chart with several columns, each column listing a variety of information. The questions require you to carry out directions involving the information given in the chart.

6) Skills and aptitudes

Performance tests effectively measure some manual skills and aptitudes. When the skill is one in which you are trained, such as typing or shorthand, you can practice. These tests are often very much like those given in business school or high school courses. For many of the other skills and aptitudes, however, no short-time preparation can be made. Skills and abilities natural to you or that you have developed throughout your lifetime are being tested.

Many of the general questions just described provide all the data needed to answer the questions and ask you to use your reasoning ability to find the answers. Your best preparation for these tests, as well as for tests of facts and ideas, is to be at your physical and mental best. You, no doubt, have your own methods of getting into an exam-taking mood and keeping "in shape." The next section lists some ideas on this subject.

IV. KINDS OF QUESTIONS

Only rarely is the "essay" question, which you answer in narrative form, used in civil service tests. Civil service tests are usually of the short-answer type. Full instructions for answering these questions will be given to you at the examination. But in case this is your first experience with short-answer questions and separate answer sheets, here is what you need to know:

1) Multiple-choice Questions

Most popular of the short-answer questions is the "multiple choice" or "best answer" question. It can be used, for example, to test for factual knowledge, ability to solve problems or judgment in meeting situations found at work.

A multiple-choice question is normally one of three types—
- It can begin with an incomplete statement followed by several possible endings. You are to find the one ending which *best* completes the statement, although some of the others may not be entirely wrong.
- It can also be a complete statement in the form of a question which is answered by choosing one of the statements listed.

- It can be in the form of a problem – again you select the best answer.

Here is an example of a multiple-choice question with a discussion which should give you some clues as to the method for choosing the right answer:

When an employee has a complaint about his assignment, the action which will *best* help him overcome his difficulty is to
- A. discuss his difficulty with his coworkers
- B. take the problem to the head of the organization
- C. take the problem to the person who gave him the assignment
- D. say nothing to anyone about his complaint

In answering this question, you should study each of the choices to find which is best. Consider choice "A" – Certainly an employee may discuss his complaint with fellow employees, but no change or improvement can result, and the complaint remains unresolved. Choice "B" is a poor choice since the head of the organization probably does not know what assignment you have been given, and taking your problem to him is known as "going over the head" of the supervisor. The supervisor, or person who made the assignment, is the person who can clarify it or correct any injustice. Choice "C" is, therefore, correct. To say nothing, as in choice "D," is unwise. Supervisors have and interest in knowing the problems employees are facing, and the employee is seeking a solution to his problem.

2) True/False Questions

The "true/false" or "right/wrong" form of question is sometimes used. Here a complete statement is given. Your job is to decide whether the statement is right or wrong.

SAMPLE: A roaming cell-phone call to a nearby city costs less than a non-roaming call to a distant city.

This statement is wrong, or false, since roaming calls are more expensive.

This is not a complete list of all possible question forms, although most of the others are variations of these common types. You will always get complete directions for answering questions. Be sure you understand *how* to mark your answers – ask questions until you do.

V. RECORDING YOUR ANSWERS

Computer terminals are used more and more today for many different kinds of exams.

For an examination with very few applicants, you may be told to record your answers in the test booklet itself. Separate answer sheets are much more common. If this separate answer sheet is to be scored by machine – and this is often the case – it is highly important that you mark your answers correctly in order to get credit.

An electronic scoring machine is often used in civil service offices because of the speed with which papers can be scored. Machine-scored answer sheets must be marked with a pencil, which will be given to you. This pencil has a high graphite content which responds to the electronic scoring machine. As a matter of fact, stray dots may register as answers, so do not let your pencil rest on the answer sheet while you are pondering the correct answer. Also, if your pencil lead breaks or is otherwise defective, ask for another.

Since the answer sheet will be dropped in a slot in the scoring machine, be careful not to bend the corners or get the paper crumpled.

The answer sheet normally has five vertical columns of numbers, with 30 numbers to a column. These numbers correspond to the question numbers in your test booklet. After each number, going across the page are four or five pairs of dotted lines. These short dotted lines have small letters or numbers above them. The first two pairs may also have a "T" or "F" above the letters. This indicates that the first two pairs only are to be used if the questions are of the true-false type. If the questions are multiple choice, disregard the "T" and "F" and pay attention only to the small letters or numbers.

Answer your questions in the manner of the sample that follows:

32. The largest city in the United States is
    A. Washington, D.C.
    B. New York City
    C. Chicago
    D. Detroit
    E. San Francisco

1) Choose the answer you think is best. (New York City is the largest, so "B" is correct.)
2) Find the row of dotted lines numbered the same as the question you are answering. (Find row number 32)
3) Find the pair of dotted lines corresponding to the answer. (Find the pair of lines under the mark "B.")
4) Make a solid black mark between the dotted lines.

VI. BEFORE THE TEST

Common sense will help you find procedures to follow to get ready for an examination. Too many of us, however, overlook these sensible measures. Indeed, nervousness and fatigue have been found to be the most serious reasons why applicants fail to do their best on civil service tests. Here is a list of reminders:

- Begin your preparation early – Don't wait until the last minute to go scurrying around for books and materials or to find out what the position is all about.
- Prepare continuously – An hour a night for a week is better than an all-night cram session. This has been definitely established. What is more, a night a week for a month will return better dividends than crowding your study into a shorter period of time.
- Locate the place of the exam – You have been sent a notice telling you when and where to report for the examination. If the location is in a different town or otherwise unfamiliar to you, it would be well to inquire the best route and learn something about the building.
- Relax the night before the test – Allow your mind to rest. Do not study at all that night. Plan some mild recreation or diversion; then go to bed early and get a good night's sleep.
- Get up early enough to make a leisurely trip to the place for the test – This way unforeseen events, traffic snarls, unfamiliar buildings, etc. will not upset you.
- Dress comfortably – A written test is not a fashion show. You will be known by number and not by name, so wear something comfortable.

- Leave excess paraphernalia at home – Shopping bags and odd bundles will get in your way. You need bring only the items mentioned in the official notice you received; usually everything you need is provided. Do not bring reference books to the exam. They will only confuse those last minutes and be taken away from you when in the test room.
- Arrive somewhat ahead of time – If because of transportation schedules you must get there very early, bring a newspaper or magazine to take your mind off yourself while waiting.
- Locate the examination room – When you have found the proper room, you will be directed to the seat or part of the room where you will sit. Sometimes you are given a sheet of instructions to read while you are waiting. Do not fill out any forms until you are told to do so; just read them and be prepared.
- Relax and prepare to listen to the instructions
- If you have any physical problem that may keep you from doing your best, be sure to tell the test administrator. If you are sick or in poor health, you really cannot do your best on the exam. You can come back and take the test some other time.

VII. AT THE TEST

The day of the test is here and you have the test booklet in your hand. The temptation to get going is very strong. Caution! There is more to success than knowing the right answers. You must know how to identify your papers and understand variations in the type of short-answer question used in this particular examination. Follow these suggestions for maximum results from your efforts:

1) Cooperate with the monitor

The test administrator has a duty to create a situation in which you can be as much at ease as possible. He will give instructions, tell you when to begin, check to see that you are marking your answer sheet correctly, and so on. He is not there to guard you, although he will see that your competitors do not take unfair advantage. He wants to help you do your best.

2) Listen to all instructions

Don't jump the gun! Wait until you understand all directions. In most civil service tests you get more time than you need to answer the questions. So don't be in a hurry. Read each word of instructions until you clearly understand the meaning. Study the examples, listen to all announcements and follow directions. Ask questions if you do not understand what to do.

3) Identify your papers

Civil service exams are usually identified by number only. You will be assigned a number; you must not put your name on your test papers. Be sure to copy your number correctly. Since more than one exam may be given, copy your exact examination title.

4) Plan your time

Unless you are told that a test is a "speed" or "rate of work" test, speed itself is usually not important. Time enough to answer all the questions will be provided, but this does not mean that you have all day. An overall time limit has been set. Divide the total time (in minutes) by the number of questions to determine the approximate time you have for each question.

5) Do not linger over difficult questions

If you come across a difficult question, mark it with a paper clip (useful to have along) and come back to it when you have been through the booklet. One caution if you do this – be sure to skip a number on your answer sheet as well. Check often to be sure that you have not lost your place and that you are marking in the row numbered the same as the question you are answering.

6) Read the questions

Be sure you know what the question asks! Many capable people are unsuccessful because they failed to *read* the questions correctly.

7) Answer all questions

Unless you have been instructed that a penalty will be deducted for incorrect answers, it is better to guess than to omit a question.

8) Speed tests

It is often better NOT to guess on speed tests. It has been found that on timed tests people are tempted to spend the last few seconds before time is called in marking answers at random – without even reading them – in the hope of picking up a few extra points. To discourage this practice, the instructions may warn you that your score will be "corrected" for guessing. That is, a penalty will be applied. The incorrect answers will be deducted from the correct ones, or some other penalty formula will be used.

9) Review your answers

If you finish before time is called, go back to the questions you guessed or omitted to give them further thought. Review other answers if you have time.

10) Return your test materials

If you are ready to leave before others have finished or time is called, take ALL your materials to the monitor and leave quietly. Never take any test material with you. The monitor can discover whose papers are not complete, and taking a test booklet may be grounds for disqualification.

VIII. EXAMINATION TECHNIQUES

1) Read the general instructions carefully. These are usually printed on the first page of the exam booklet. As a rule, these instructions refer to the timing of the examination; the fact that you should not start work until the signal and must stop work at a signal, etc. If there are any *special* instructions, such as a choice of questions to be answered, make sure that you note this instruction carefully.

2) When you are ready to start work on the examination, that is as soon as the signal has been given, read the instructions to each question booklet, underline any key words or phrases, such as *least, best, outline, describe* and the like. In this way you will tend to answer as requested rather than discover on reviewing your paper that you *listed without describing*, that you selected the *worst* choice rather than the *best* choice, etc.

3) If the examination is of the objective or multiple-choice type – that is, each question will also give a series of possible answers: A, B, C or D, and you are called upon to select the best answer and write the letter next to that answer on your answer paper – it is advisable to start answering each question in turn. There may be anywhere from 50 to 100 such questions in the three or four hours allotted and you can see how much time would be taken if you read through all the questions before beginning to answer any. Furthermore, if you come across a question or group of questions which you know would be difficult to answer, it would undoubtedly affect your handling of all the other questions.

4) If the examination is of the essay type and contains but a few questions, it is a moot point as to whether you should read all the questions before starting to answer any one. Of course, if you are given a choice – say five out of seven and the like – then it is essential to read all the questions so you can eliminate the two that are most difficult. If, however, you are asked to answer all the questions, there may be danger in trying to answer the easiest one first because you may find that you will spend too much time on it. The best technique is to answer the first question, then proceed to the second, etc.

5) Time your answers. Before the exam begins, write down the time it started, then add the time allowed for the examination and write down the time it must be completed, then divide the time available somewhat as follows:
    - If 3-1/2 hours are allowed, that would be 210 minutes. If you have 80 objective-type questions, that would be an average of 2-1/2 minutes per question. Allow yourself no more than 2 minutes per question, or a total of 160 minutes, which will permit about 50 minutes to review.
    - If for the time allotment of 210 minutes there are 7 essay questions to answer, that would average about 30 minutes a question. Give yourself only 25 minutes per question so that you have about 35 minutes to review.

6) The most important instruction is to *read each question* and make sure you know what is wanted. The second most important instruction is to *time yourself properly* so that you answer every question. The third most important instruction is to *answer every question*. Guess if you have to but include something for each question. Remember that you will receive no credit for a blank and will probably receive some credit if you write something in answer to an essay question. If you guess a letter – say "B" for a multiple-choice question – you may have guessed right. If you leave a blank as an answer to a multiple-choice question, the examiners may respect your feelings but it will not add a point to your score. Some exams may penalize you for wrong answers, so in such cases *only*, you may not want to guess unless you have some basis for your answer.

7) Suggestions
    a. Objective-type questions
        1. Examine the question booklet for proper sequence of pages and questions
        2. Read all instructions carefully
        3. Skip any question which seems too difficult; return to it after all other questions have been answered
        4. Apportion your time properly; do not spend too much time on any single question or group of questions

5. Note and underline key words – *all, most, fewest, least, best, worst, same, opposite,* etc.
6. Pay particular attention to negatives
7. Note unusual option, e.g., unduly long, short, complex, different or similar in content to the body of the question
8. Observe the use of "hedging" words – *probably, may, most likely,* etc.
9. Make sure that your answer is put next to the same number as the question
10. Do not second-guess unless you have good reason to believe the second answer is definitely more correct
11. Cross out original answer if you decide another answer is more accurate; do not erase until you are ready to hand your paper in
12. Answer all questions; guess unless instructed otherwise
13. Leave time for review

b. Essay questions
   1. Read each question carefully
   2. Determine exactly what is wanted. Underline key words or phrases.
   3. Decide on outline or paragraph answer
   4. Include many different points and elements unless asked to develop any one or two points or elements
   5. Show impartiality by giving pros and cons unless directed to select one side only
   6. Make and write down any assumptions you find necessary to answer the questions
   7. Watch your English, grammar, punctuation and choice of words
   8. Time your answers; don't crowd material

8) Answering the essay question

Most essay questions can be answered by framing the specific response around several key words or ideas. Here are a few such key words or ideas:

M's: manpower, materials, methods, money, management
P's: purpose, program, policy, plan, procedure, practice, problems, pitfalls, personnel, public relations

   a. Six basic steps in handling problems:
      1. Preliminary plan and background development
      2. Collect information, data and facts
      3. Analyze and interpret information, data and facts
      4. Analyze and develop solutions as well as make recommendations
      5. Prepare report and sell recommendations
      6. Install recommendations and follow up effectiveness

   b. Pitfalls to avoid
      1. *Taking things for granted* – A statement of the situation does not necessarily imply that each of the elements is necessarily true; for example, a complaint may be invalid and biased so that all that can be taken for granted is that a complaint has been registered

2. *Considering only one side of a situation* – Wherever possible, indicate several alternatives and then point out the reasons you selected the best one
3. *Failing to indicate follow up* – Whenever your answer indicates action on your part, make certain that you will take proper follow-up action to see how successful your recommendations, procedures or actions turn out to be
4. *Taking too long in answering any single question* – Remember to time your answers properly

IX. AFTER THE TEST

Scoring procedures differ in detail among civil service jurisdictions although the general principles are the same. Whether the papers are hand-scored or graded by machine we have described, they are nearly always graded by number. That is, the person who marks the paper knows only the number – never the name – of the applicant. Not until all the papers have been graded will they be matched with names. If other tests, such as training and experience or oral interview ratings have been given, scores will be combined. Different parts of the examination usually have different weights. For example, the written test might count 60 percent of the final grade, and a rating of training and experience 40 percent. In many jurisdictions, veterans will have a certain number of points added to their grades.

After the final grade has been determined, the names are placed in grade order and an eligible list is established. There are various methods for resolving ties between those who get the same final grade – probably the most common is to place first the name of the person whose application was received first. Job offers are made from the eligible list in the order the names appear on it. You will be notified of your grade and your rank as soon as all these computations have been made. This will be done as rapidly as possible.

People who are found to meet the requirements in the announcement are called "eligibles." Their names are put on a list of eligible candidates. An eligible's chances of getting a job depend on how high he stands on this list and how fast agencies are filling jobs from the list.

When a job is to be filled from a list of eligibles, the agency asks for the names of people on the list of eligibles for that job. When the civil service commission receives this request, it sends to the agency the names of the three people highest on this list. Or, if the job to be filled has specialized requirements, the office sends the agency the names of the top three persons who meet these requirements from the general list.

The appointing officer makes a choice from among the three people whose names were sent to him. If the selected person accepts the appointment, the names of the others are put back on the list to be considered for future openings.

That is the rule in hiring from all kinds of eligible lists, whether they are for typist, carpenter, chemist, or something else. For every vacancy, the appointing officer has his choice of any one of the top three eligibles on the list. This explains why the person whose name is on top of the list sometimes does not get an appointment when some of the persons lower on the list do. If the appointing officer chooses the second or third eligible, the No. 1 eligible does not get a job at once, but stays on the list until he is appointed or the list is terminated.

X. HOW TO PASS THE INTERVIEW TEST

The examination for which you applied requires an oral interview test. You have already taken the written test and you are now being called for the interview test – the final part of the formal examination.

You may think that it is not possible to prepare for an interview test and that there are no procedures to follow during an interview. Our purpose is to point out some things you can do in advance that will help you and some good rules to follow and pitfalls to avoid while you are being interviewed.

What is an interview supposed to test?

The written examination is designed to test the technical knowledge and competence of the candidate; the oral is designed to evaluate intangible qualities, not readily measured otherwise, and to establish a list showing the relative fitness of each candidate – as measured against his competitors – for the position sought. Scoring is not on the basis of "right" and "wrong," but on a sliding scale of values ranging from "not passable" to "outstanding." As a matter of fact, it is possible to achieve a relatively low score without a single "incorrect" answer because of evident weakness in the qualities being measured.

Occasionally, an examination may consist entirely of an oral test – either an individual or a group oral. In such cases, information is sought concerning the technical knowledges and abilities of the candidate, since there has been no written examination for this purpose. More commonly, however, an oral test is used to supplement a written examination.

Who conducts interviews?

The composition of oral boards varies among different jurisdictions. In nearly all, a representative of the personnel department serves as chairman. One of the members of the board may be a representative of the department in which the candidate would work. In some cases, "outside experts" are used, and, frequently, a businessman or some other representative of the general public is asked to serve. Labor and management or other special groups may be represented. The aim is to secure the services of experts in the appropriate field.

However the board is composed, it is a good idea (and not at all improper or unethical) to ascertain in advance of the interview who the members are and what groups they represent. When you are introduced to them, you will have some idea of their backgrounds and interests, and at least you will not stutter and stammer over their names.

What should be done before the interview?

While knowledge about the board members is useful and takes some of the surprise element out of the interview, there is other preparation which is more substantive. It *is* possible to prepare for an oral interview – in several ways:

1) Keep a copy of your application and review it carefully before the interview

This may be the only document before the oral board, and the starting point of the interview. Know what education and experience you have listed there, and the sequence and dates of all of it. Sometimes the board will ask you to review the highlights of your experience for them; you should not have to hem and haw doing it.

2) Study the class specification and the examination announcement

Usually, the oral board has one or both of these to guide them. The qualities, characteristics or knowledges required by the position sought are stated in these documents. They offer valuable clues as to the nature of the oral interview. For example, if the job involves supervisory responsibilities, the announcement will usually indicate that knowledge of modern supervisory methods and the qualifications of the candidate as a supervisor will be tested. If so, you can expect such questions, frequently in the form of a hypothetical situation which you are expected to solve. NEVER go into an oral without knowledge of the duties and responsibilities of the job you seek.

3) Think through each qualification required

Try to visualize the kind of questions you would ask if you were a board member. How well could you answer them? Try especially to appraise your own knowledge and background in each area, *measured against the job sought*, and identify any areas in which you are weak. Be critical and realistic – do not flatter yourself.

4) Do some general reading in areas in which you feel you may be weak

For example, if the job involves supervision and your past experience has NOT, some general reading in supervisory methods and practices, particularly in the field of human relations, might be useful. Do NOT study agency procedures or detailed manuals. The oral board will be testing your understanding and capacity, not your memory.

5) Get a good night's sleep and watch your general health and mental attitude

You will want a clear head at the interview. Take care of a cold or any other minor ailment, and of course, no hangovers.

What should be done on the day of the interview?

Now comes the day of the interview itself. Give yourself plenty of time to get there. Plan to arrive somewhat ahead of the scheduled time, particularly if your appointment is in the fore part of the day. If a previous candidate fails to appear, the board might be ready for you a bit early. By early afternoon an oral board is almost invariably behind schedule if there are many candidates, and you may have to wait. Take along a book or magazine to read, or your application to review, but leave any extraneous material in the waiting room when you go in for your interview. In any event, relax and compose yourself.

The matter of dress is important. The board is forming impressions about you – from your experience, your manners, your attitude, and your appearance. Give your personal appearance careful attention. Dress your best, but not your flashiest. Choose conservative, appropriate clothing, and be sure it is immaculate. This is a business interview, and your appearance should indicate that you regard it as such. Besides, being well groomed and properly dressed will help boost your confidence.

Sooner or later, someone will call your name and escort you into the interview room. *This is it.* From here on you are on your own. It is too late for any more preparation. But remember, you asked for this opportunity to prove your fitness, and you are here because your request was granted.

What happens when you go in?

The usual sequence of events will be as follows: The clerk (who is often the board stenographer) will introduce you to the chairman of the oral board, who will introduce you to the other members of the board. Acknowledge the introductions before you sit down. Do not be surprised if you find a microphone facing you or a stenotypist sitting by. Oral interviews are usually recorded in the event of an appeal or other review.

Usually the chairman of the board will open the interview by reviewing the highlights of your education and work experience from your application – primarily for the benefit of the other members of the board, as well as to get the material into the record. Do not interrupt or comment unless there is an error or significant misinterpretation; if that is the case, do not hesitate. But do not quibble about insignificant matters. Also, he will usually ask you some question about your education, experience or your present job – partly to get you to start talking and to establish the interviewing "rapport." He may start the actual questioning, or turn it over to one of the other members. Frequently, each member undertakes the questioning on a particular area, one in which he is perhaps most competent, so you can expect each member to participate in the examination. Because time is limited, you may also expect some rather abrupt switches in the direction the questioning takes, so do not be upset by it. Normally, a board member will not pursue a single line of questioning unless he discovers a particular strength or weakness.

After each member has participated, the chairman will usually ask whether any member has any further questions, then will ask you if you have anything you wish to add. Unless you are expecting this question, it may floor you. Worse, it may start you off on an extended, extemporaneous speech. The board is not usually seeking more information. The question is principally to offer you a last opportunity to present further qualifications or to indicate that you have nothing to add. So, if you feel that a significant qualification or characteristic has been overlooked, it is proper to point it out in a sentence or so. Do not compliment the board on the thoroughness of their examination – they have been sketchy, and you know it. If you wish, merely say, "No thank you, I have nothing further to add." This is a point where you can "talk yourself out" of a good impression or fail to present an important bit of information. Remember, *you close the interview yourself*.

The chairman will then say, "That is all, Mr. _____, thank you." Do not be startled; the interview is over, and quicker than you think. Thank him, gather your belongings and take your leave. Save your sigh of relief for the other side of the door.

How to put your best foot forward

Throughout this entire process, you may feel that the board individually and collectively is trying to pierce your defenses, seek out your hidden weaknesses and embarrass and confuse you. Actually, this is not true. They are obliged to make an appraisal of your qualifications for the job you are seeking, and they want to see you in your best light. Remember, they must interview all candidates and a non-cooperative candidate may become a failure in spite of their best efforts to bring out his qualifications. Here are 15 suggestions that will help you:

1) Be natural – Keep your attitude confident, not cocky

If you are not confident that you can do the job, do not expect the board to be. Do not apologize for your weaknesses, try to bring out your strong points. The board is interested in a positive, not negative, presentation. Cockiness will antagonize any board member and make him wonder if you are covering up a weakness by a false show of strength.

2) Get comfortable, but don't lounge or sprawl

Sit erectly but not stiffly. A careless posture may lead the board to conclude that you are careless in other things, or at least that you are not impressed by the importance of the occasion. Either conclusion is natural, even if incorrect. Do not fuss with your clothing, a pencil or an ashtray. Your hands may occasionally be useful to emphasize a point; do not let them become a point of distraction.

3) Do not wisecrack or make small talk

This is a serious situation, and your attitude should show that you consider it as such. Further, the time of the board is limited – they do not want to waste it, and neither should you.

4) Do not exaggerate your experience or abilities

In the first place, from information in the application or other interviews and sources, the board may know more about you than you think. Secondly, you probably will not get away with it. An experienced board is rather adept at spotting such a situation, so do not take the chance.

5) If you know a board member, do not make a point of it, yet do not hide it

Certainly you are not fooling him, and probably not the other members of the board. Do not try to take advantage of your acquaintanceship – it will probably do you little good.

6) Do not dominate the interview

Let the board do that. They will give you the clues – do not assume that you have to do all the talking. Realize that the board has a number of questions to ask you, and do not try to take up all the interview time by showing off your extensive knowledge of the answer to the first one.

7) Be attentive

You only have 20 minutes or so, and you should keep your attention at its sharpest throughout. When a member is addressing a problem or question to you, give him your undivided attention. Address your reply principally to him, but do not exclude the other board members.

8) Do not interrupt

A board member may be stating a problem for you to analyze. He will ask you a question when the time comes. Let him state the problem, and wait for the question.

9) Make sure you understand the question

Do not try to answer until you are sure what the question is. If it is not clear, restate it in your own words or ask the board member to clarify it for you. However, do not haggle about minor elements.

10) Reply promptly but not hastily

A common entry on oral board rating sheets is "candidate responded readily," or "candidate hesitated in replies." Respond as promptly and quickly as you can, but do not jump to a hasty, ill-considered answer.

11) Do not be peremptory in your answers

A brief answer is proper – but do not fire your answer back. That is a losing game from your point of view. The board member can probably ask questions much faster than you can answer them.

12) Do not try to create the answer you think the board member wants

He is interested in what kind of mind you have and how it works – not in playing games. Furthermore, he can usually spot this practice and will actually grade you down on it.

13) Do not switch sides in your reply merely to agree with a board member

Frequently, a member will take a contrary position merely to draw you out and to see if you are willing and able to defend your point of view. Do not start a debate, yet do not surrender a good position. If a position is worth taking, it is worth defending.

14) Do not be afraid to admit an error in judgment if you are shown to be wrong

The board knows that you are forced to reply without any opportunity for careful consideration. Your answer may be demonstrably wrong. If so, admit it and get on with the interview.

15) Do not dwell at length on your present job

The opening question may relate to your present assignment. Answer the question but do not go into an extended discussion. You are being examined for a *new* job, not your present one. As a matter of fact, try to phrase ALL your answers in terms of the job for which you are being examined.

Basis of Rating

Probably you will forget most of these "do's" and "don'ts" when you walk into the oral interview room. Even remembering them all will not ensure you a passing grade. Perhaps you did not have the qualifications in the first place. But remembering them will help you to put your best foot forward, without treading on the toes of the board members.

Rumor and popular opinion to the contrary notwithstanding, an oral board wants you to make the best appearance possible. They know you are under pressure – but they also want to see how you respond to it as a guide to what your reaction would be under the pressures of the job you seek. They will be influenced by the degree of poise you display, the personal traits you show and the manner in which you respond.

ABOUT THIS BOOK

This book contains tests divided into Examination Sections. Go through each test, answering every question in the margin. We have also attached a sample answer sheet at the back of the book that can be removed and used. At the end of each test look at the answer key and check your answers. On the ones you got wrong, look at the right answer choice and learn. Do not fill in the answers first. Do not memorize the questions and answers, but understand the answer and principles involved. On your test, the questions will likely be different from the samples. Questions are changed and new ones added. If you understand these past questions you should have success with any changes that arise. Tests may consist of several types of questions. We have additional books on each subject should more study be advisable or necessary for you. Finally, the more you study, the better prepared you will be. This book is intended to be the last thing you study before you walk into the examination room. Prior study of relevant texts is also recommended. NLC publishes some of these in our Fundamental Series. Knowledge and good sense are important factors in passing your exam. Good luck also helps. So now study this Passbook, absorb the material contained within and take that knowledge into the examination. Then do your best to pass that exam.

EXAMINATION SECTION

EXAMINATION SECTION

TEST 1

DIRECTIONS: Each question or incomplete statement is followed by several suggested answers or completions. Select the one that BEST answers the question or completes the statement. *PRINT THE LETTER OF THE CORRECT ANSWER IN THE SPACE AT THE RIGHT.*

Questions 1-23

DIRECTIONS: The meters in Questions 1 through 23 are read as illustrated below.

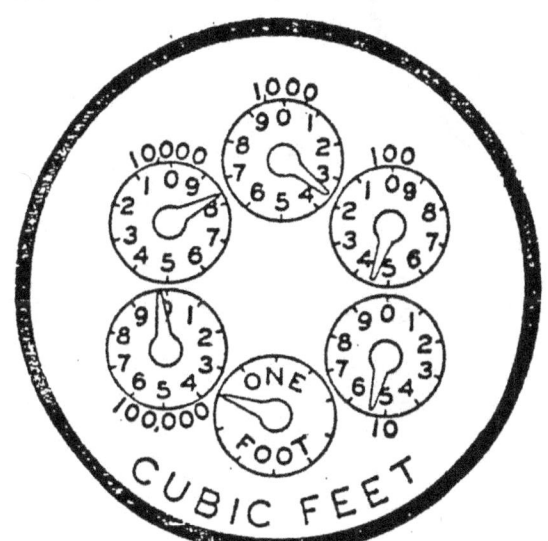

Dial   10 reads   5
Dial   100 reads   40
Dial   1,000 reads   300
Dial   10,000 reads   8,000
Dial   100,000 reads   90,000

The reading is 98,345 cubic feet

(Assume that the maximum consumption between consecutive meter readings was less than 100,000 cubic feet.)

1. The *correct* reading for the meter shown in the diagram above is, most nearly,
   A. 1,408 cubic feet
   B. 8,041 cubic feet
   C. 19,152 cubic feet
   D. 25,191 cubic feet

1._____

2. The *correct* reading for the meter shown in the diagram above is, most nearly,
   A. 54,545 cubic feet
   B. 65,656 cubic feet
   C. 545,454 cubic feet
   D. 656,565 cubic feet

2._____

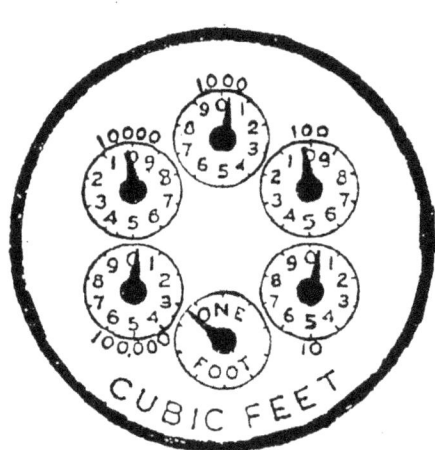

3. The *correct* reading for the meter shown in the diagram above is, most nearly,
   A. 0 cubic feet
   B. 1 cubic foot
   C. 8 cubic feet
   D. 111,111 cubic feet

3._____

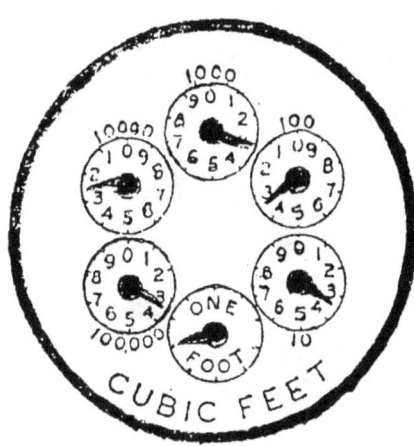
Meter A

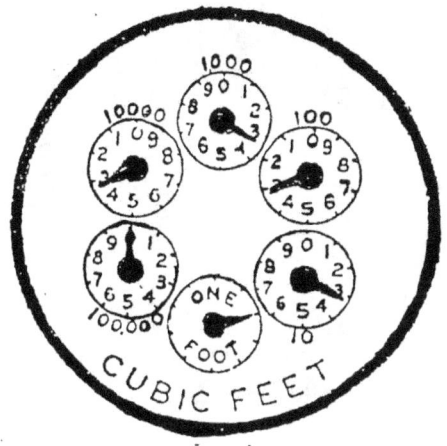
Meter B

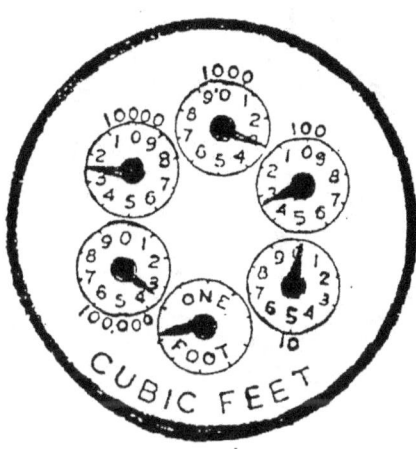
Meter C

Meter D

4. In the diagram above, the meter which *most nearly* indicates a reading of 33,333 cubic feet is Meter

    A. A   B. B   C. C   D. D

4._____

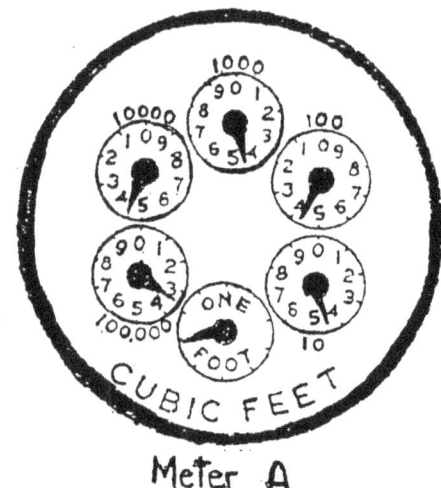
Meter A

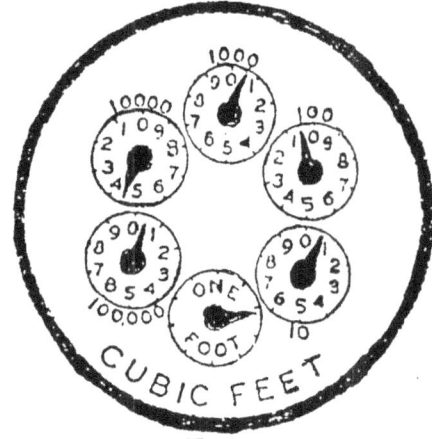
Meter B

Meter C

Meter D

5. In the diagram above, the meter which *most nearly* indicates a reading of four thousand cubic feet is Meter

    A. A   B. B   C. C   D. D

5._____

6. On the basis of the meter reading shown in the diagram above, a Meter Reader calculated that the consumption between the previous reading and this reading was 9,356 cubic feet.
   Based on this information, the previous meter reading should have been, most nearly,
   A. 59,331 cubic feet
   B. 78,043 cubic feet
   C. 88,154 cubic feet
   D. 677,521 cubic feet

6._____

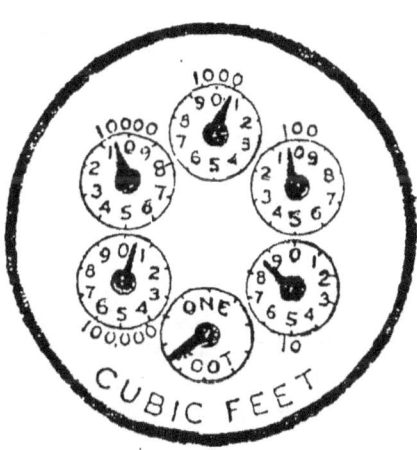

7. On the basis of the meter reading shown in the diagram above, a Meter Reader calculated that the consumption between the previous meter reading and this reading was 1,356 cubic feet.
   Based on this information, the previous meter reading should have been, most nearly,
   A. 0 cubic feet
   B. 3,164 cubic feet
   C. 11,348 cubic feet
   D. 98,652 cubic feet

7._____

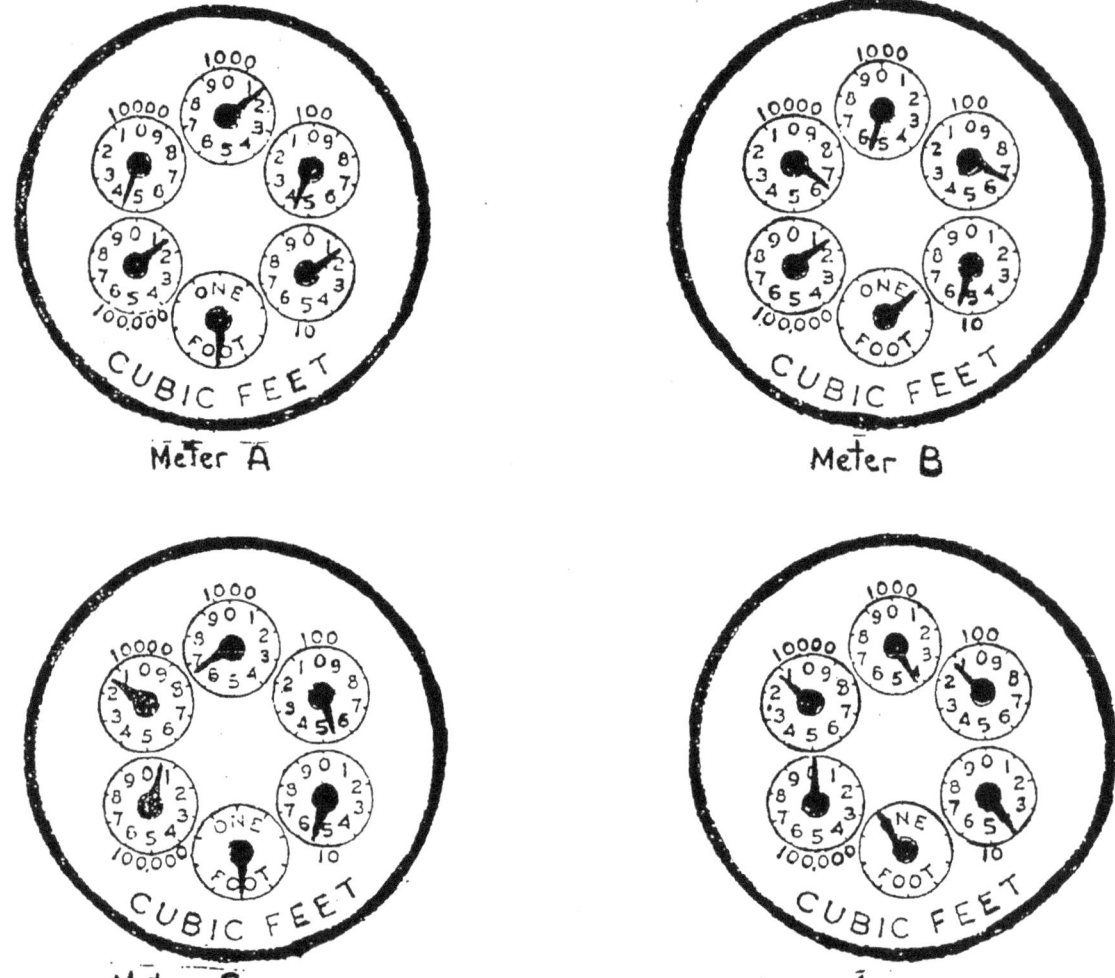

8. A Meter Reader notes that the previous reading for a certain meter was 15,353 cubic feet. After observing the present meter reading, he calculates that the meter indicates the consumption between readings was most nearly 1,212 cubic feet.
The *one* of the diagrams above which most nearly shows the *present* meter reading is Meter

    A. A   B. B   C. C   D. D

8._____

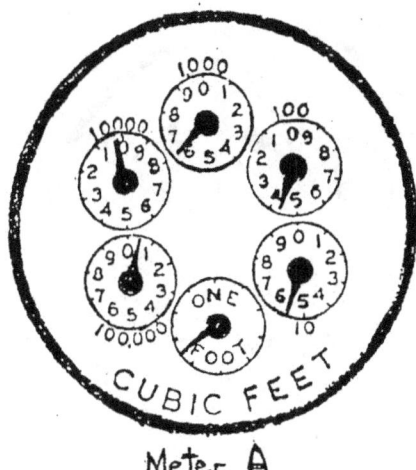
Meter A

Meter B

Meter C

Meter D

9. A Meter Reader notes that the previous reading for a certain meter was 645 cubic feet. After observing the present meter reading, he calculates that the meter indicates the consumption between readings was most nearly 721 cubic feet.
The *one* of the diagrams above which most nearly shows the *present* meter reading is Meter

   A. A   B. B   C. C   D. D

9._____

Previous Reading

Present Reading

10. The present reading and the previous reading of a certain meter are illustrated above. The amount consumed between meter readings was, most nearly,
    A. 9,824 cubic feet
    B. 17,813 cubic feet
    C. 18,814 cubic feet
    D. 19,824 cubic feet

10._____

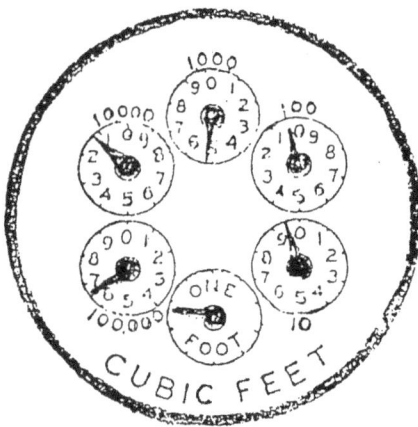
Previous Reading

Present Reading

11. The present reading and the previous reading of a certain meter are illustrated above. The amount consumed between meter readings was, most nearly,
    A. 2,025 cubic feet
    B. 3,136 cubic feet
    C. 4,686 cubic feet
    D. 6,313 cubic feet

11._____

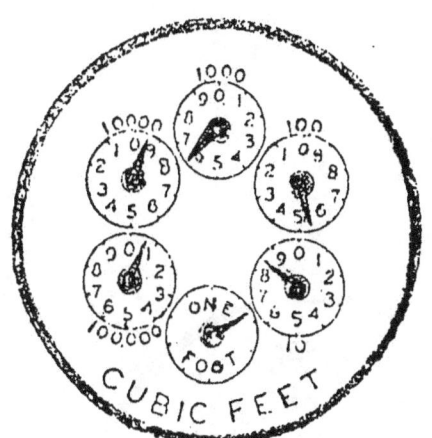
Previous Reading

Present Reading

12. The present reading and the previous reading of a certain meter are illustrated above. The amount consumed between meter readings was, most nearly,

    A. 314 cubic feet   B. 646 cubic feet
    C. 1,646 cubic feet   D. 9,354 cubic feet

12._____

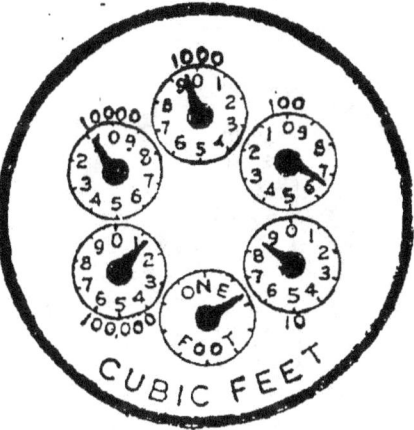
Meter A

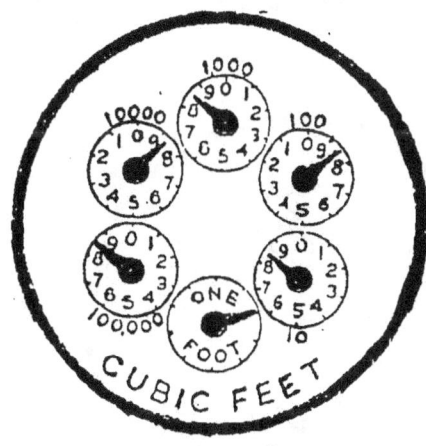
Meter B

Meter C

Meter D

13. Of the meters illustrated above, the *one* which has the *HIGHEST* reading is Meter

    A. A   B. B   C. C   D. D

13._____

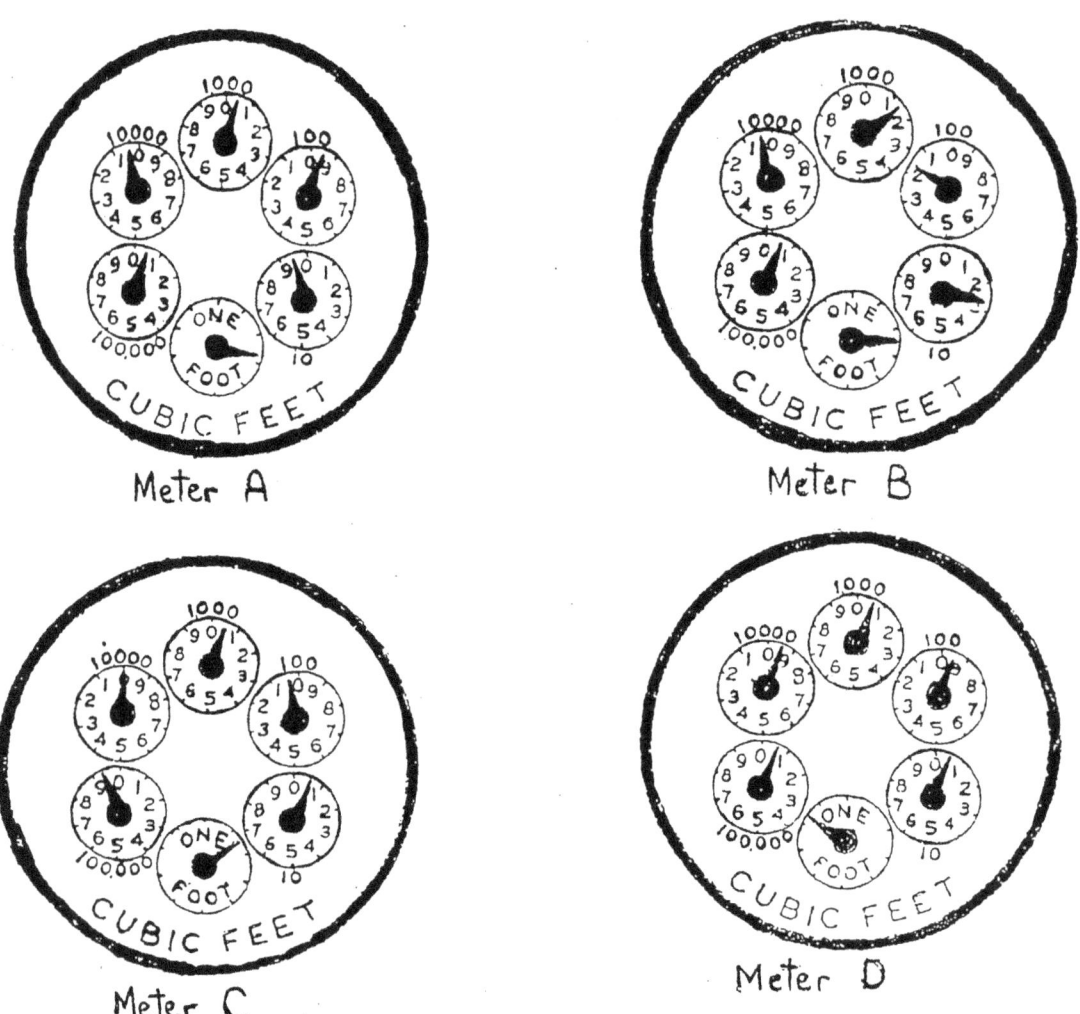

14. Of the meters illustrated above, the *one* which has the LOWEST reading is Meter

   A. A   B. B   C. C   D. D

14._____

15. If there are 7-1/2 gallons in a cubic foot of water, then the number of gallons indicated by the meter shown above is, most nearly,
    A. 149.5   B. 256   C. 3,600   D. 1117.5

15._____

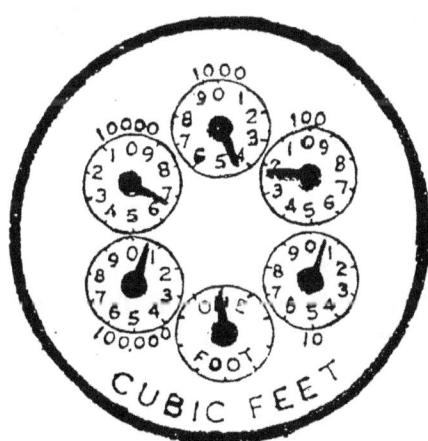

16. If there are 7-1/2 gallons in a cubic foot of water, then the number of gallons indicated by the meter shown above is, most nearly,
    A. 5,154   B. 48,150   C. 6,420   D. 86

16._____

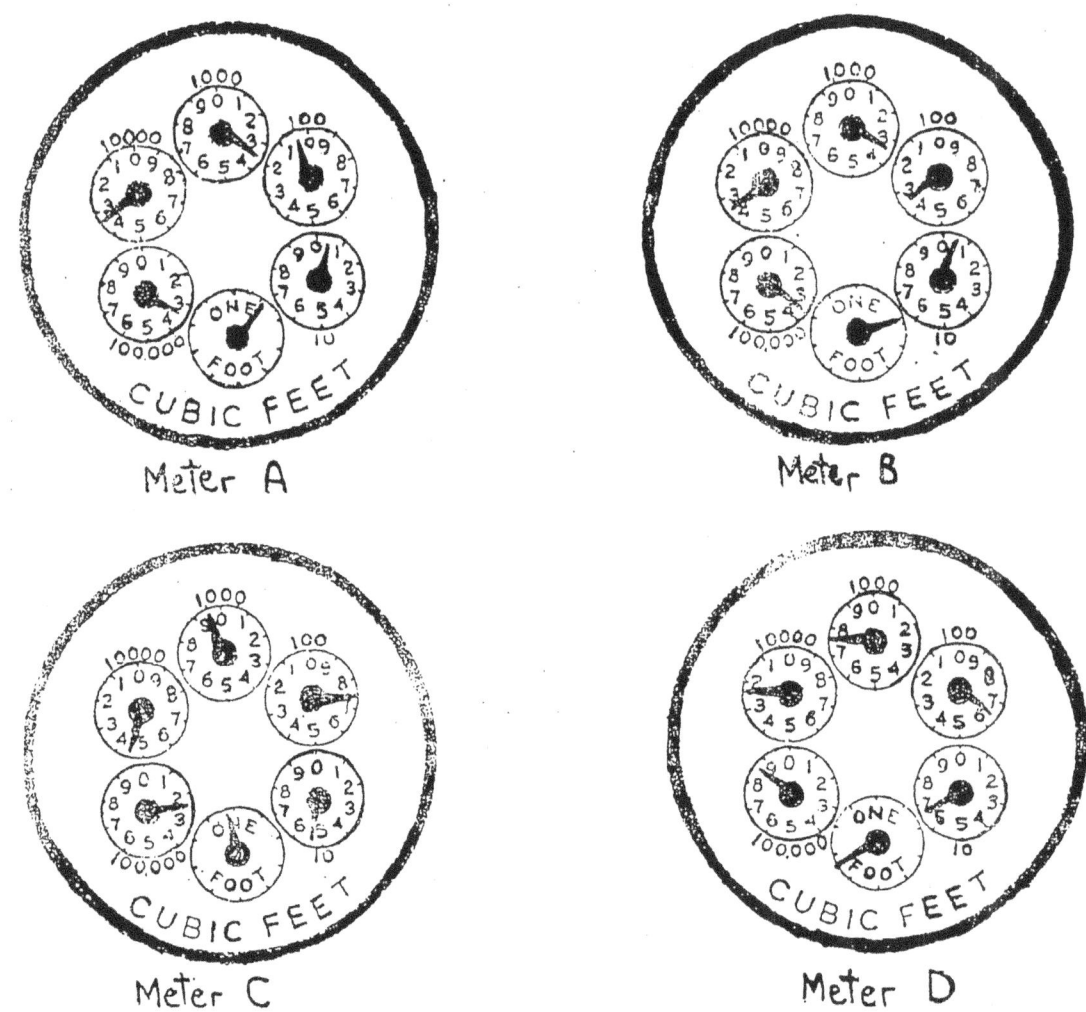

17. If there are 7-1/2 gallons in a cubic foot of water, the meter illustrated above which shows a reading equivalent to 249,750 gallons is Meter
   A. A   B. B   C. C   D. D

17._____

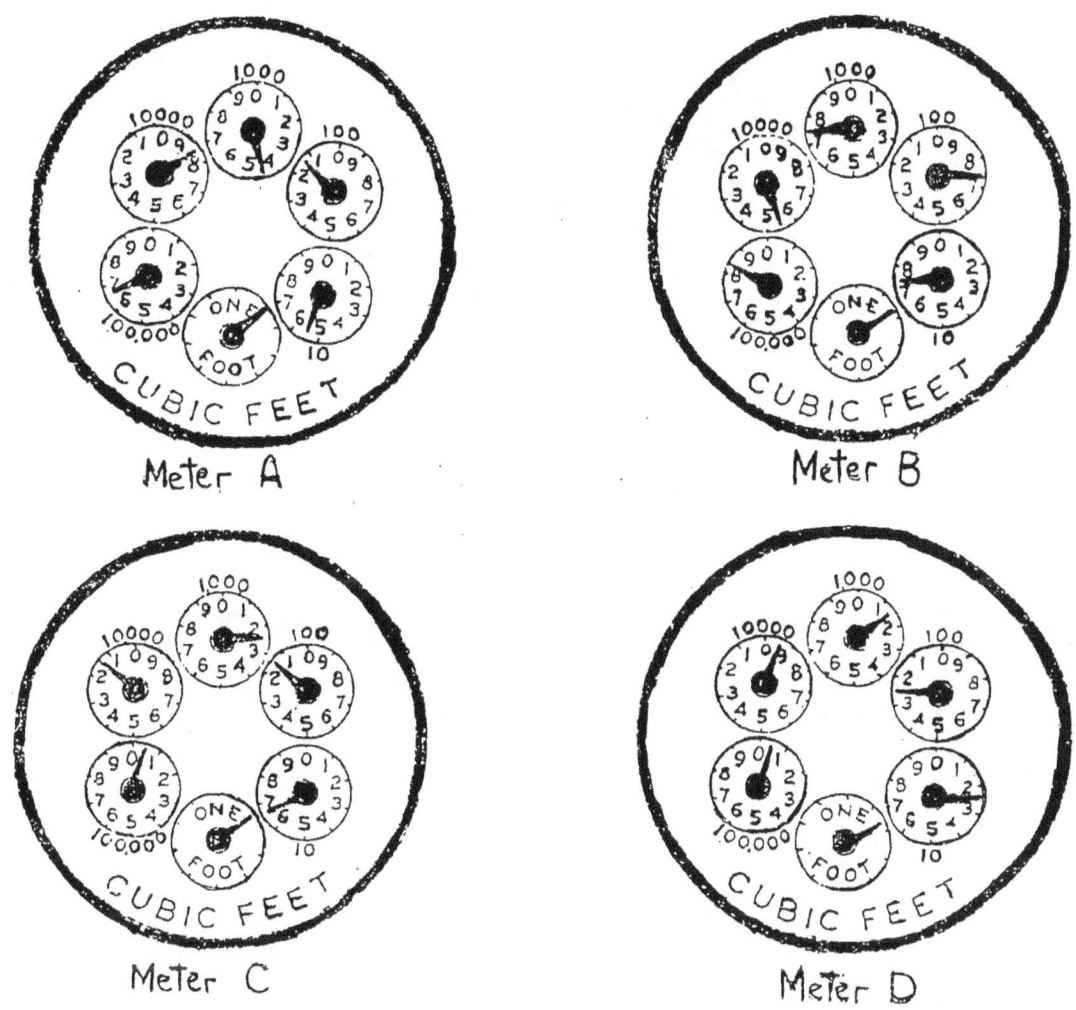

18. If there are 7-1/2 gallons in a cubic foot of water, the meter illustrated above which shows a reading equivalent to 68,415 gallons is Meter   18._____
    A. A   B. B   C. C   D. D

Questions 19-20

DIRECTIONS: Answer Questions 19 and 20 on the basis of the illustration below.

19. For each 1/4 revolution of the hand on the dial marked 100,000, the hand on the dial marked 100 revolves
    A. 25 times
    B. 250 times
    C. 2,500 times
    D. 25,000 times

20. When the hand on the dial marked 1,000 moves from numeral 4 to numeral 9, the hand turns through an angle of
    A. 90°   B. 108°   C. 120°   D. 180°

21. For the purpose of billing consumers, water consumption is measured by water meters. These water meters, most commonly, measure units of
    A. velocity   B. volume   C. area   D. weight

22. When 1-5/8, 3-3/4, 6-1/3 and 9-1/2 are added, the resulting sum is
    A. 21-1/8   B. 21-1/6   C. 21-5/24   D. 21-1/4

23. When 946-1/2 is subtracted from 1,035-1/4, the result is
    A. 87-1/4   B. 87-3/4   C. 88-1/4   D. 88-3/4

24. When 39 is multiplied by 697, the result is
    A. 8,364   B. 26,283   C. 27,183   D. 28,003

25. When 16.074 is divided by .045, the result is
    A. 3.6   B. 35.7   C. 357.2   D. 3,572

Questions 26-30

DIRECTIONS: Answer Questions 26 to 30 on the basis of the information given in the table below.

Meter Readings in Cubic Feet

Date of Reading	Meter 1	Meter 2	Meter 3	Meter 4	Meter 5
Dec. 31, 2003	12,416	88,990	64,312	26,985	30,057
June 30, 2004	23,094	98,806	71,527	27,336	30,057
Dec. 31, 2004	33,011	07,723	79,292	27,848	30,618
June 30, 2005	42,907	16,915	87,208	28,286	31,247
Dec. 31, 2005	52,603	26,456	95,244	28,742	31,740

Note: The maximum readings of each of the above meters is 99,999 cubic feet. Above that reading the meters start registering from zero.
Note: Assume that the maximum consumption between consecutive readings is less than 100,000 cubic feet.

26. The meter which showed the *LOWEST* consumption for the period June 30, 2005 to December 31, 2005 is Meter
    A. 2 B. 3 C. 4 D. 5

27. The amount consumed between June 30, 2004 and December 31, 2004 by the consumers metered by Meter 2 is
    A. 7,723 cubic feet
    B. 8,917 cubic feet
    C. 91,083 cubic feet
    D. 107,723 cubic feet

28. The meter which showed the *GREATEST* consumption over the time period December 31, 2003 to December 31, 2005 is Meter
    A. 1 B. 2 C. 3 D. 4

29. The meter which showed *exactly* the same consumption for 2005 as in 2004 is Meter
    A. 1 B. 2 C. 4 D. 5

30. The meter which shows *exactly twice* as much consumption in 2005 as compared to the consumption in 2004 is Meter
    A. 1 B. 3 C. 4 D. 5

KEY (CORRECT ANSWERS)

1. B	11. B	21. B
2. A	12. B	22. C
3. A	13. C	23. D
4. D	14. A	24. C
5. B	15. D	25. C
6. A	16. B	26. C
7. D	17. A	27. B
8. B	18. D	28. A
9. B	19. B	29. B
10. C	20. D	30. D

TEST 2

DIRECTIONS: Each question or incomplete statement is followed by several suggested answers or completions. Select the one that BEST answers the question or completes the statement. *PRINT THE LETTER OF THE CORRECT ANSWER IN THE SPACE AT THE RIGHT.*

1. A certain consumer used 5% more in 1996 than he did in 1995. If his consumption for 1996 was 8,375 cubic feet, the amount he consumed in 1995 was, most nearly,
    A. 9,014 cubic feet
    B. 8,816 cubic feet
    C. 7,976 cubic feet
    D. 6,776 cubic feet

    1._____

2. Assume that a meter reads 40,172 cubic feet and the previous reading was 29,186 cubic feet. If the charge is 23 cents per 100 cubic feet or any fraction thereof, the bill for the amount used since the previous meter reading should be
    A. $25.07
    B. $25.26
    C. $25.27
    D. $25.30

    2._____

3. Each of a group of fifteen Meter Readers read an average of 62 meters a day in a certain 5-day work week. A total of 5,115 meters are read by this group the following week.
   The total number of meters read in the second week as compared to the first week shows a
    A. 10% increase
    B. 15% increase
    C. 20% increase
    D. 5% decrease

    3._____

4. A Meter Reader discovers that a large, vicious-looking, unleashed dog is in a cellar where he is assigned to read the meter. The dog snarls whenever the Meter Reader approaches the cellar, but the dog's owner assures the reader that the dog has never bitten anyone.
   Of the following, the *BEST* course of action for the Meter Reader to take is to
    A. enter the cellar and ignore the dog
    B. find a large object to carry to scare the dog
    C. try to make friends with the dog
    D. politely ask the owner to restrain the dog

    4._____

5. While on an assignment to read the meter at a certain building, a Meter Reader discovers evidence indicating that the meter was illegally tampered with.
   Of the following, the *BEST* course of action for him to take is to
    A. summon the Police Department immediately and have them check for fingerprints
    B. make a note to report this to his Department
    C. issue a summons to the person responsible for the meter without giving an explanation
    D. not report anything unless he has conclusive evidence that the meter was indeed illegally tampered with

    5._____

6. A Meter Reader finds that there has been a serious fire at one of the buildings where he is assigned to read the meter. The city has placed danger signs on the building, stating that the building is condemned.
Of the following, the BEST course of action for the Meter Reader to take is to
    A. enter the building and read the meter quickly before anyone interferes
    B. first put a note on the door explaining his presence, and then read the meter
    C. estimate the meter reading on the basis of past bills without entering the building
    D. note in his assignment book that the premise is condemned and not enter the building

6._____

7. At a certain business where a Meter Reader is assigned to read the meter, a woman refuses him entry because her husband is not home at the time.
Of the following, the BEST course of action for the Meter Reader to take is to
    A. ask her to read the meter for him
    B. flash his credentials and then force his way in to read the meter
    C. summon the police and explain that she is obstructing official city business
    D. note the circumstances in his assignment book so that the Department can arrange another appointment

7._____

8. While a Meter Reader is reading the meter at a small business, the owner angrily complains about the high cost of services in the city.
Of the following, the BEST course of action for the Meter Reader to take is to
    A. tell the owner to be quiet and have respect for city representatives
    B. try to persuade the owner to take a more reasonable point of view
    C. listen courteously until the owner finishes talking
    D. ignore the owner's comments

8._____

9. After reading the meter at a small business, a Meter Reader is approached by the owner who offers him some money if he would move several pieces of furniture.
Of the following, the BEST course of action for the Meter Reader to take is to
    A. courteously refuse the job
    B. do the job for the money as long as he has enough time so that it doesn't interfere with his regular assignment
    C. do the job but refuse any payment
    D. phone his supervisor first and let him decide whether the request is reasonable

9._____

10. While a Meter Reader is in the field, a newspaper reporter stops him and asks for information regarding rate increases for utility consumption.
Of the following, the BEST course of action for the Meter Reader to take is to
    A. ignore the newspaper reporter
    B. refer him to the main office for the Department's official information
    C. tell the reporter anything he wants to know, but warn him that the information is not official
    D. give the newspaper man wrong information in order to discourage him from further questioning

10._____

11. A Meter Reader is assigned to read a meter in a tightly covered meter pit which has not been opened for some time. Because the meter pit is located in a chemical plant, he suspects that the accumulated air in the pit may not have enough oxygen or may be explosive.
Of the following, the FIRST safety precaution for him to take is to
    A. open the pit and test the air with a lighted match
    B. open the pit cover and allow the pit to be ventilated
    C. enter the pit slowly and sniff the air for any telltale odor
    D. lower his lighted flashlight into the pit to test for visibility

11._____

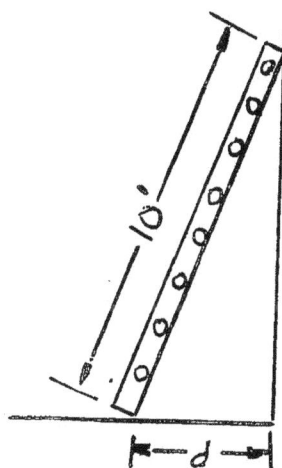

12. A Meter Reader is required to climb the 10' ladder shown above.
Of the following, the SAFEST distance (d) that the base of the ladder should be from the wall is
    A. 1/2 foot   B. 1-1/2 feet   C. 2-1/2 feet   D. 3-1/2 feet

12._____

13. A Meter Reader's hands become frostbitten on a cold winter day.
Of the following, the BEST first-aid treatment is to
    A. apply warm towels to his hands and give him a warm drink
    B. place his hands in cold saltwater
    C. have him rub his hands together over a warm stove
    D. place his hands in cold water and give him a warm drink

13._____

Questions 14-15

DIRECTIONS: Questions 14 and 15 are to be answered in accordance with the paragraph below.

Meters shall be set or reset so that they may be easily examined and read. In all premises where the utility supply is to be fully metered, the meter shall be set within three feet of the building or vault wall at point of entry of the service pipe. The service pipe between meter control valve and meter shall be kept exposed. When a building is situated back of the building line or conditions exist in a building that prevent the setting of the meter at a point of entry, the meter may be set outside of the building in a proper water-tight and frost-proof pit or meter box, or at another location approved by the Deputy Commissioner, Assistant to Commissioner or the Chief Inspector.

14. According to the above paragraph, a meter should be set
    A. at a point in the building convenient to the owner
    B. within three feet of the building wall
    C. in back of the building
    D. where the district inspector thinks is best

14._____

15. According to the above paragraph, one of the conditions imposed when a meter is permitted to be installed outside of a building is that the meter must be installed
    A. between the service pipe and the meter control valve
    B. within three feet of the point of entry of the service pipe
    C. in a water-tight enclosure
    D. above ground in a frost-proof box

15._____

Questions 16-19

DIRECTIONS: Questions 16 through 19 refer to the diagram of the dials of a meter shown below.

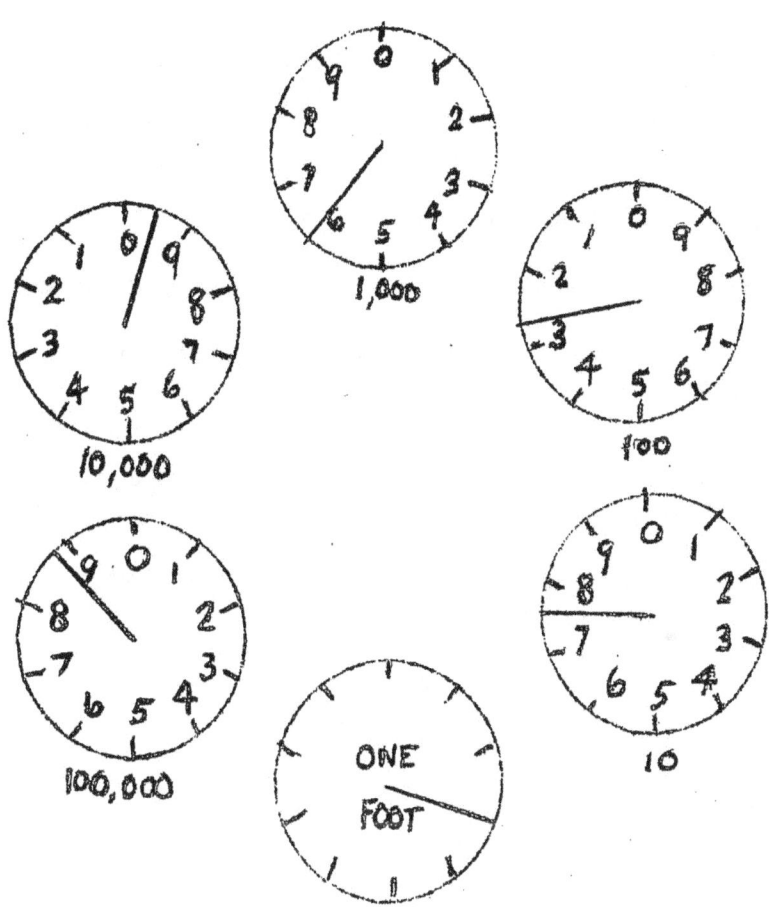

16. The *CORRECT* reading of the meter, in cubic feet, is 16._____
    A. 72,698   B. 89,627   C. 90,637   D. 80,637

17. For each complete revolution of the hand on the dial marked 10,000, the hand on the dial marked 10 revolves _____ times. 17._____
    A. 3   B. 20   C. 300   D. 1,000

18. The statement *MOST NEARLY CORRECT* is that the hands on _____ rotate in a _____ direction. 18._____
    A. all the dials; clockwise
    B. all the dials; counter-clockwise
    C. the dials marked 10, 1,000 and 100,000; clockwise
    D. the dials marked 10, 1,000 and 100,000; counter-clockwise

19. If the hand on the 1,000 dial was exactly on the number 7, and then moved to the number 8, the hand on the 100 dial would move
    A. one space clockwise
    B. completely around the dial and stop in the same place it was originally
    C. one space counter-clockwise
    D. one or more spaces, depending on flow

19.____

20. Assume that a meter reads 50,631 cubic feet and the previous reading was 39,842 cubic feet.
    If the charge is 23 cents per 100 cubic feet or any fraction thereof, the bill for the amount consumed since the previous meter reading will be, most nearly,
    A. $24.22   B. $24.38   C. $24.84   D. $24.95

20.____

21. At a certain premises, consumption was 4 percent higher in 1995 than it was in 1994.
    If the consumption for 1995 was 9,740 cubic feet, then the consumption for 1994 was, most nearly,
    A. 9,320   B. 9,350   C. 9,365   D. 9,390

21.____

22. While a building owner is escorting a Meter Reader to the cellar of the building, the building owner slips on the cellar stairs and falls and breaks his leg.
    Of the following types of first-aid procedures, the one that is BEST for the Meter Reader to take in this case is to
    A. move the victim to a warm place
    B. place the victim's leg in cold water to minimize swelling
    C. keep the victim still and try to keep him warm
    D. give the victim a stimulant to drink

22.____

23. A Meter Reader finds that the sidewalk cellar door is open at a premises in which he is supposed to read the meter.
    Of the following, the BEST course of action for the Meter Reader to take is to
    A. enter the cellar and read the meter before anyone interferes
    B. obtain authorization from a responsible person at the premises before entering the cellar
    C. make some noise by banging on the door to determine if an unrestrained dog is on the premises and, if not, enter the cellar
    D. make an estimate of the meter reading to save the time and effort of searching through the cellar

23.____

24. While reading meters at a premise, a Meter Reader is confronted by the owner who asks him to clean out the clogged drain of a kitchen sink.
    Of the following, the BEST course of action for the Meter Reader to take is to
    A. comply with the request for a small fee, if it does not interfere with the day's assignment
    B. attempt the job for non-monetary compensation
    C. recommend the Roto-Rooter man
    D. politely refuse to comply with the request

24.____

25. Of the following, the indication that would cause the MOST suspicion that 25._____
    a meter may have been illegally tampered with is
    A. a seal wire broken by corrosion
    B. fresh wrench marks on a meter outlet valve
    C. a new coat of paint on the meter and surrounding pipes
    D. missing glass on the meter register

KEY (CORRECT ANSWERS)

1. C	6. D	11. B	16. B	21. C
2. D	7. D	12. C	17. D	22. C
3. A	8. C	13. A	18. C	23. B
4. D	9. A	14. B	19. B	24. D
5. B	10. B	15. C	20. C	25. D

TEST 3

DIRECTIONS: Each question or incomplete statement is followed by several suggested answers or completions. Select the one that BEST answers the question or completes the statement. *PRINT THE LETTER OF THE CORRECT ANSWER IN THE SPACE AT THE RIGHT.*

Questions 1-2

DIRECTIONS: Questions 1 and 2 are to be answered on the basis of the diagrams of the meter dials shown below.

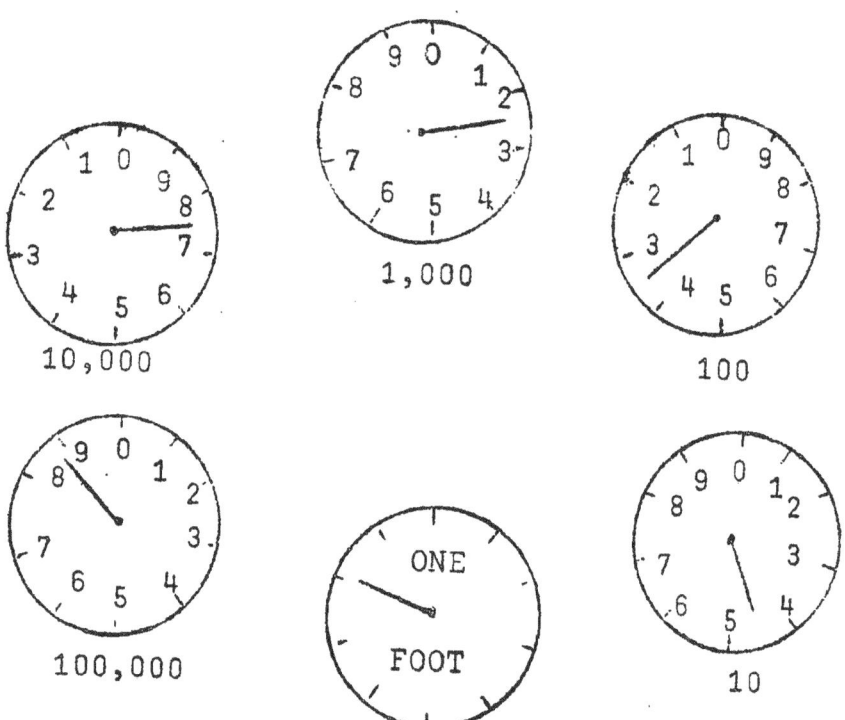

1. The *CORRECT* meter reading, in cubic feet, is
   A. 43,278   B. 54,389   C. 87,234   D. 98,345

   1._____

2. For each half revolution of the hand on the 10,000 dial, the hand on the indicator marked 10 will revolve _____ times.
   A. 50   B. 500   C. 5,000   D. 50,000

   2._____

3. The *MAIN* reason for placing a seal on a meter is to
   A. keep a record of the dates on which the meter was inspected
   B. prevent contamination
   C. indicate tampering with the meter
   D. show that it is an approved meter

   3._____

4. A Meter Reader who is reading a meter in the cellar of an apartment house is approached by a man who appears to be intoxicated. The man makes abusive remarks about government employees, calling them lazy and dishonest.
   In this situation, the Meter Reader should
   A. attempt to persuade the man that he is mistaken in his opinions
   B. call for a policeman to have the man arrested for abusing a government employee in the performance of his duty
   C. make his readings without answering the man
   D. ask the man for proof of his charges

4._____

5. While reading a meter, a Meter Reader was engaged in conversation by a talkative woman. When the Meter Reader completed his reading, the woman was still talking and obviously had much more to say. The Meter Reader skillfully ended the conversation, politely said goodbye and left.
   The Meter Reader's method of handling this situation was
   A. *proper*; Meter Readers should never talk to the public except about business
   B. *not proper*; the Meter Reader should not have permitted the woman to start the conversation in the first place
   C. *proper*; Meter Readers should not waste time in idle conversation
   D. *not proper*; the Meter Reader should have waited until the woman was finished in order to create good will for the department

5._____

6. A Meter Reader, checking the seals on a meter in the basement of an apartment house, is approached by a man who asks what he is doing. The Meter Reader tells the man that he is from a utility company and that he is checking the meter. The man then demands to see his credentials.
   The Meter Reader should
   A. show his identification card to the man
   B. ignore the man and continue his work
   C. find out whether the man is a tenant or superintendent of the building
   D. tell the man that he should call the utility company if he is not satisfied with the explanation

6._____

7. While reading a meter, a Meter Reader notices some defective plumbing and advises the owner of the condition. The owner offers the job to the Meter Reader, to be done on his free time.
   In this situation, the Meter Reader should
   A. agree to do the work if he has the spare time and wants the additional money
   B. refuse to do the work, explaining that it would be a violation of the department's policy
   C. refuse the work but recommend a reliable plumber
   D. advise the owner how he could do the work himself

7._____

8. A Meter Reader, while reading the meter in a restaurant, is invited by the owner to have lunch "on the house."
   The Meter Reader should
   A. accept the invitation but select the cheapest meal on the menu
   B. refuse the invitation but thank the owner for the offer
   C. accept the invitation but refuse any alcoholic beverages
   D. refuse the invitation and tell the owner that he can afford to pay for his meals

8.____

9. A meter reads 87,463 cubic feet. If the previous reading was 17,377 cubic feet and the rate charged is 15 cents per 100 cubic feet, the bill for consumption during this period is about
   A. $45.00   B. $65.00   C. $85.00   D. $105.00

9.____

Questions 10-12

DIRECTIONS: Questions 10 to 12 relate to the diagram of the meter below.

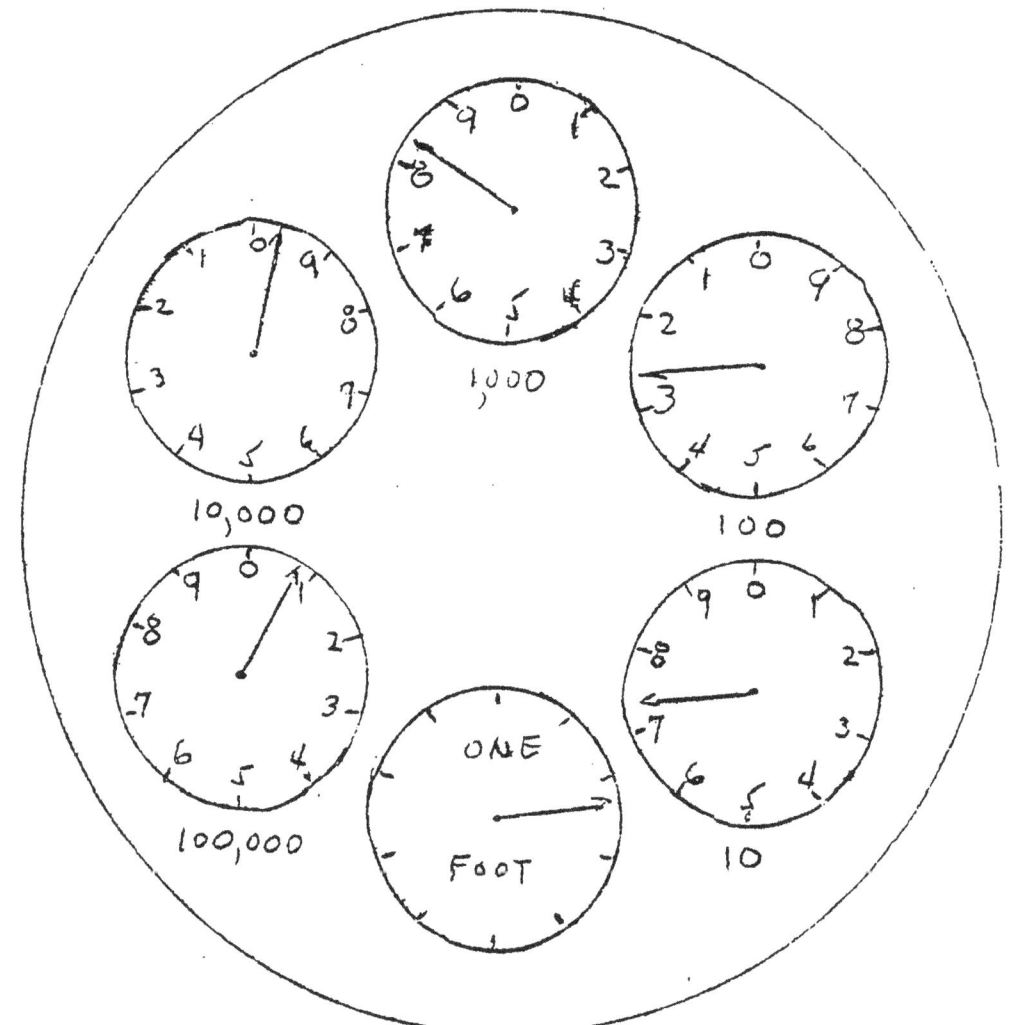

10. The *CORRECT* reading of the meter is, in cubic feet, 10.____
    A. 198,277   B. 108,383   C. 99,388   D. 9,827

11. In the operation of the meter, the rotation of the indicator on the dial 11.____
    marked ONE
    A. is in a clockwise direction
    B. is in a counter-clockwise direction
    C. is first in a clockwise, then counter-clockwise direction
    D. cannot be determined from the diagram

12. The *LARGEST* quantity that can be recorded by the meter is, in cubic 12.____
    feet,
    A. 10,000,000   B. 1,000,000   C. 100,000   D. 10,000

13. You notice that a meter is not registering even though the utility is turned 13.____
    on. You should
    A. inform your supervisor
    B. install a new meter yourself
    C. repair the meter yourself
    D. shut off the utility

14. You find the seal broken on a meter you are reading. You should 14.____
    A. order the consumer to reseal the meter at once
    B. report the fact to your supervisor
    C. reseal the meter yourself and say nothing, hoping you can catch
       the culprit
    D. test the meter yourself, making the consumer bear the cost

15. Of the following, a meter's *most important* advantage is that it 15.____
    A. can be easily discarded if it doesn't work
    B. is easy to keep in repair
    C. is inexpensive to install
    D. offers a fair basis for billing a consumer

Questions 16-20

DIRECTIONS: Questions 16 to 20 are based on the meters on the next page.

16. The *correct* reading for Meter A is: 16.____
    A. 3,888   B. 92,777   C. 203,888   D. 292,777

17. The *correct* reading for Meter B is: 17.____
    A. 8,999   B. 88,990   C. 99,000   D. 188,990

18. The *correct* reading for Meter C is: 18.____
    A. 9,826   B. 110,937   C. 5,009,826   D. 6,110,937

19. The *correct* reading for Meter D is: 19.____
    A. 5,609   B. 945,989   C. 994,598   D. 9,945,989

5 (#3)

20. Assume that in Meter A the correct reading is 4,331 cubic feet. The previous reading was 84,622 cubic feet. Consumption, in cubic feet, between the two readings has been

    A. 4,331   B. 19,709   C. 80,291   D. 88,953

20._____

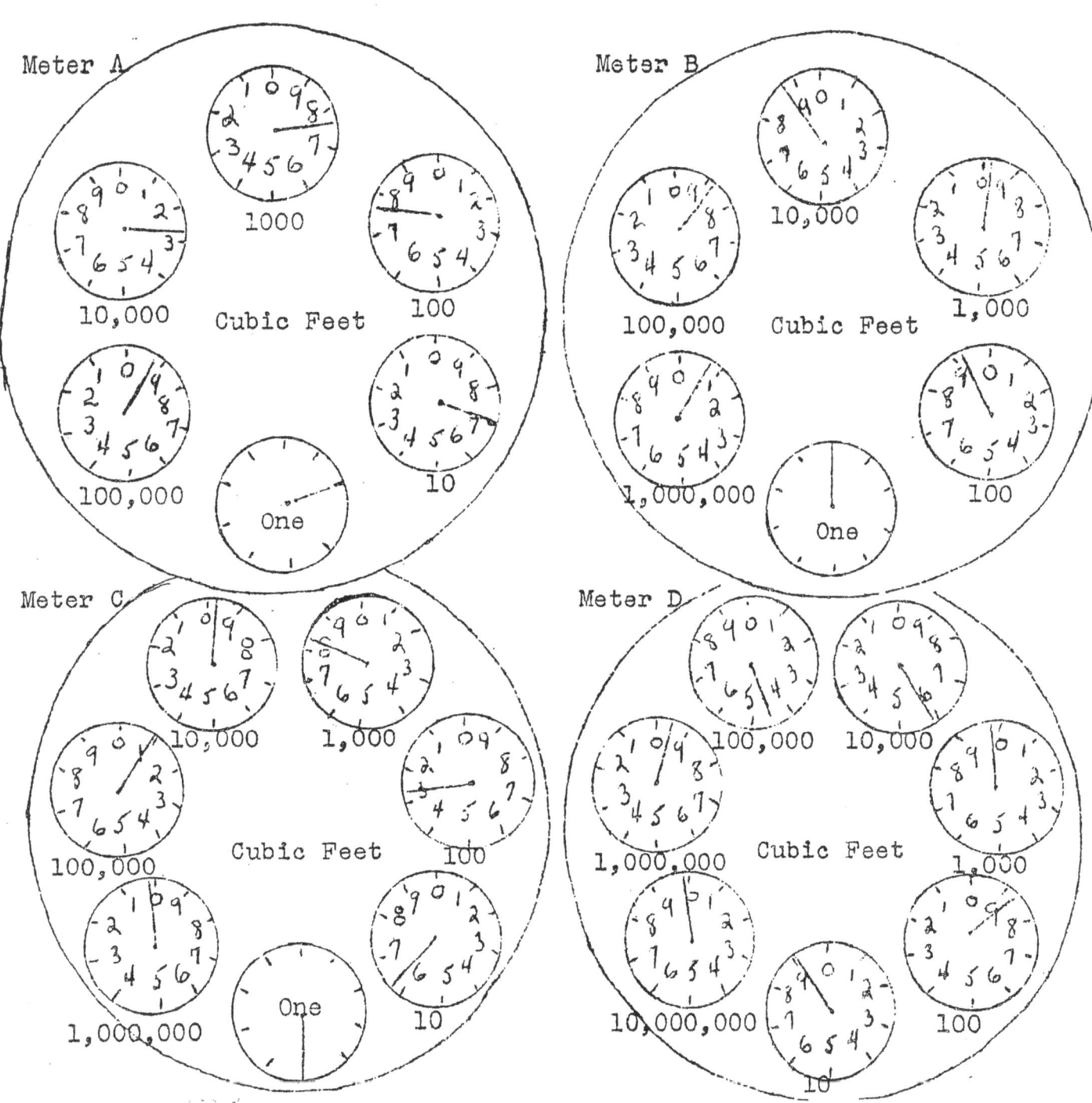

Questions 21-25

DIRECTIONS: Answer questions 21 to 25 *only* on the basis of the information contained in the following paragraph.

Meter rates at present are 15 cents per 100 cubic feet. The meter rates remained the same from 1970 to the end of 2001. Beginning January 1, 2002, these rates were increased a flat 50 percent.

21. The charge for 98,300 cubic feet at present is
   A. $98.30   B. $122.87   C. 147.45
   D. cannot be calculated from the facts given

21._____

22. The charge for 69,340 cubic feet at present is
   A. $69.34   B. $86.67   C. $104.01
   D. cannot be calculated from the facts given

22._____

23. The charge in 2001 for 87,420 cubic feet was
   A. $87.42   B. $133.13   C. $110.27
   D. cannot be calculated from the facts given

23._____

24. The charge in 1970 for 51,220 cubic feet was
   A. $51.22   B. $64.02   C. $76.83
   D. cannot be calculated from the facts given

24._____

25. A meter reads 81,400 cubic feet on January 1, 2002 and 21,800 cubic feet on January 1, 2003.
The charge for consumption between the two readings is
   A. $60.60   B. $89.40   C. $75.00
   D. cannot be calculated from the facts given

25._____

26. The meter reading shown in the following sketch, in cubic feet, is
   A. 373,591   B. 68,449   C. 37,359   D. 173,359

26._____

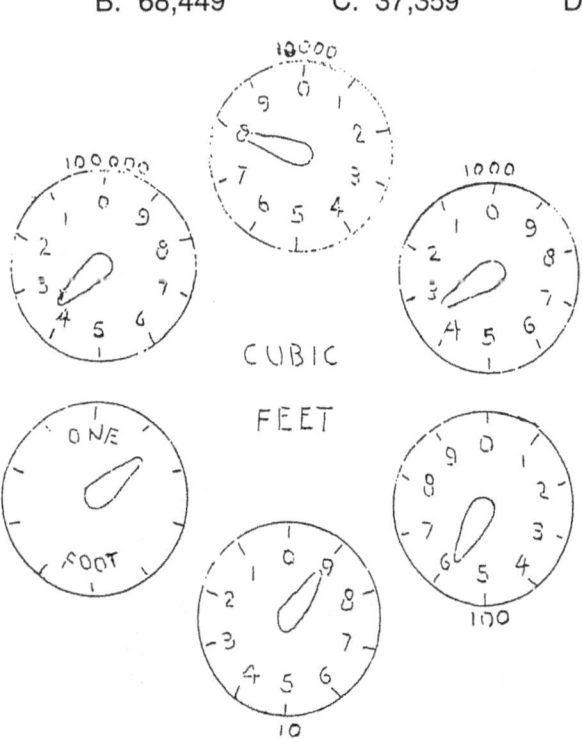

7 (#3)

27. Assume that the current meter reading on the preceding diagram is 8,947 cubic feet. The last reading was 81,732 cubic feet.
    It is obvious that
    A. consumption amounted to 72,785 cubic feet
    B. the meter has been tampered with
    C. the meter is not recording properly
    D. consumption amounted to 27,215 cubic feet

27._____

28. After you have read a meter, the owner tells you that he will be unable to pay the bill on time and asks what will happen.
    You *should* tell him that
    A. you just read the meter; after that, it is up to the office
    B. you will report the matter to your superior
    C. if he fails to pay before the end of next month he will be charged interest on the bill
    D. the city's financial position is not good and he should make every effort to pay the bill

28._____

29. A Meter Reader, sent to obtain meter readings, is refused admission to the premises.
    The Meter Reader's next step should be to
    A. recommend that service to the premises be shut off
    B. report the refusal to his superior for further action
    C. obtain the assistance of the police to force access to the meter
    D. recommend using the average consumption for the last three periods to determine the current charge

29._____

30. On an inspection of a meter in a commercial building, you see a man in the basement working on an oil burner. You do not know his identity or whether he is authorized to work in the building.
    The most reasonable thing to do is to
    A. pay no attention to the man and take the meter reading
    B. ignore him, but include a brief statement about him in your report
    C. challenge the man and obtain his identity
    D. watch him carefully to determine if his behavior is proper

30._____

KEY (CORRECT ANSWERS)

1. C	11. B	21. C
2. B	12. C	22. C
3. C	13. A	23. A
4. C	14. B	24. A
5. C	15. D	25. A
6. A	16. B	26. C
7. B	17. B	27. D
8. B	18. A	28. C
9. D	19. D	29. B
10. D	20. B	30. A

EXAMINATION SECTION
TEST 1

DIRECTIONS: Each question or incomplete statement is followed by several suggested answers or completions. Select the one that BEST answers the question or completes the statement. *PRINT THE LETTER OF THE CORRECT ANSWER IN THE SPACE AT THE RIGHT.*

1. The charge for metered water is 52 1/2 cents per hundred cubic feet, with a minimum charge of $21 per annum. Of the following, the smallest water usage in hundred cubic feet that would result in a charge GREATER than the minimum is

   A. 39   B. 40   C. 41   D. 42

   1.____

2. The symbol shown at the right on a piping drawing represents a _____ elbow.
   A. turned up
   B. union
   C. long radius
   D. reducing

   2.____

3. A gate valve on a piping drawing should be shown as

   3.____

4. A cap on a piping drawing should be shown as

   4.____

5. The annual frontage rent on a one-story building 40 ft. in length is $73.50. For each additional story, $5.25 per annum is added to the frontage rent. For demolition, the charge for wetting down is 3/8 of the annual frontage charge.
   The charge for wetting down a building six stories in height, with a 40 ft. frontage, is MOST NEARLY

   A. $36.90   B. $37.10   C. $37.20   D. $37.40

   5.____

6. On an inspector's *meter reading report,* you see the notation MNP.
   This means that the meter is NOT

   A. pointing correctly
   B. piped properly
   C. equipped with a pointer
   D. in place

   6.____

7. The highest fixture in a building is 60 ft. above the level of the main in the street.
   If the water pressure in the main is 40 psi, then the water pressure at the fixture when no water is flowing in the building is, in psi, MOST NEARLY

   A. 0   B. 40   C. 26   D. 14

   7.____

31

8. Where city water is needed to prime a pump used to pump brine, the one of the following that MUST be installed to prevent contamination of the city water is a(n)

    A. vacuum breaker B. indirect source of supply
    C. check valve   D. pressure regulator

9. The device used to stop the flow of water into a roof tank when it is full is a(n)

    A. pressure relay B. automatic ball stop
    C. swing valve   D. overflow pipe

10. The factor that differentiates between the definition of an air conditioning system and the definition of a refrigeration system is the

    A. means of cooling
    B. size of the system
    C. temperature to which the system cools
    D. refrigerant used in cooling

11. Metering of the city water supply to an air conditioning system is required when

    A. there is no water conserving device in the system
    B. the supply of water to the system is in excess of 1.5 G.P.M.
    C. the system does not have an automatic water regulating valve
    D. the rating of the system is greater than 1/3 ton

12. As stated in the Rules, an air conditioning system using city water is required to be equipped with an approved water conserving device when its rated capacity is in excess of _____ ton(s).

    A. 1   B. 1 1/2   C. 2   D. 2 1/2

13. In estimating the probable quantity of water that will be used in a building, the rates of flow in all fixtures are compared to that of a specific fixture taken as *one fixture unit*. This fixture is a

    A. wash basin (lavatory)   B. water closet (flush tank)
    C. sink (kitchen)   D. shower (stall)

14. Of the following, the one that is NOT considered a *water conserving device* as used in *air conditioning and refrigeration* is a(n)

    A. evaporative condenser   B. water cooling tower
    C. spray pond   D. well

15. One ton of refrigeration is equivalent to the removal of heat at the rate of _____ BTU/hr.

    A. 10,000   B. 11,000   C. 12,000   D. 13,000

16. In the rating of electric air conditioning systems, one horsepower of the compressor motor is equivalent to _____ ton(s) of air conditioning.

    A. 1   B. 1 1/2   C. 2   D. 2 1/2

17. A relief valve is required on a direct water connection to a refrigeration system when the   17._____

    A. pressure of the refrigerant is more than 5 pounds above maximum water pressure
    B. refrigerating system contains more than 20 pounds of refrigerant
    C. refrigerating system has no check valve on the water line
    D. refrigerating system has a check valve on the water line

18. Where a building is used for both business and dwelling purposes, and the hot water   18._____
    supply to both uses comes from a central hot water system,

    A. there need be only one hot water meter to serve both uses
    B. the business use must have a separate hot water meter
    C. a single hot water meter may be used only where the business use requires a meter smaller than 2"
    D. a single hot water meter may be used only when the meter is a compound meter

19. The new building code requires that all water used in the construction of buildings 75 ft.   19._____
    or six stories or more in height shall be metered.
    This differs from the *Rules* used by the Bureau of Water Register, which requires metering for the construction of buildings _____ or more stories in height.

    A. 75 ft. or seven   B. 60 ft. or six
    C. six   D. seven

20. A cold water meter may be repaired on the premises ONLY if it is   20._____

    A. not a disc type meter
    B. on a construction site
    C. 3-inch in size or larger
    D. used for fire service lines

21. Of the following, the one that would be considered a water service pipe is a   21._____

    A. pipe extending from the public water main to the house control valve
    B. by-pass pipe used to cut out a defective meter temporarily
    C. pipe running from main distribution line to a large refrigeration unit
    D. pipe used to return steam condensate to a boiler

22. House control valves for water may be_____ type.   22._____

    A. only gate   B. gate or swing
    C. swing or globe   D. gate or globe

23. With respect to a meter installation in a new building, the piping from the inlet valve to the   23._____
    outlet valve of the meter should be

    A. at most one standard size larger
    B. at most two standard sizes larger
    C. at most one standard size smaller
    D. of the same size

24. A hot water meter may   24._____

    A. not be repaired on the premises
    B. be repaired on the premises only if it is a disc type meter

C. be repaired on the premises only if it is a current type meter
D. be repaired on the premises only if it is a compound type meter

25. The SMALLEST approved current type meter is

    A. 1 1/2" B. 2" C. 3" D. 4"

26. A by-pass around a meter would MOST likely be permitted when

    A. water flow may occasionally be very low
    B. a test tee is required
    C. there may be great fluctuation in the water flow
    D. the building has only one source of supply

27. Water hammer MOST frequently will occur in a pipe when

    A. the diameter of the pipe is suddenly enlarged
    B. a valve is shut suddenly
    C. the pipe is improperly hung
    D. weather is cold and ice forms in the pipe

28. The PRINCIPAL advantage a gate valve has over a globe valve is that the gate valve

    A. is easier to attach in a line than a globe valve
    B. is smaller than the globe valve
    C. permits flow in only one direction
    D. does not obstruct the flow of water as much as a globe valve does

29. Of the following, the BEST method of preventing a *cross connection* is by use of a(n)

    A. air gap   B. check valve
    C. pressure regulator   D. vent tube

30. The MOST common method of preventing siphonage of the contents of a water closet back into the Water supply pipe is by means of a

    A. built-in P trap   B. vacuum breaker
    C. ball cock   D. float valve

31. A complaint is received of inadequate water pressure in the top story of a building.
    Of the following, the one that would be LEAST likely to be a cause of this condition is

    A. an undersized pipe   B. a corroded pipe
    C. water hammer   D. an air lock

32. It has frequently been recommended that all one-family homes be metered.
    The MAIN basis for this recommendation is that this practice will

    A. distribute the cost of water supply over the entire population more equitably
    B. reduce the amount of water wasted by homeowners
    C. maintain adequate water pressure in the system
    D. result in people who can afford it, paying for the water

33. Where water is being pumped, an air chamber may be used in connection with the pump. The reason for use of the air chamber is to

   A. prevent loss of prime in the pump
   B. increase the capacity of the pump
   C. store water for peak hour use
   D. equalize fluctuations in flow of water

33._____

34. It is necessary to prime a booster pump which is in good condition either automatically or by hand, when the pump is a _____ pump.

   A. centrifugal   B. rotary
   C. piston   D. positive displacement

34._____

35. In very tall buildings, where water is pumped to a storage tank on the roof, pressure of water on the lower floors may be controlled by all but one of the following methods. The one NOT used is

   A. installation of an auxiliary tank at a lower floor
   B. a pressure relief valve at the lower floor
   C. a pressure reduction valve at the lower floor
   D. by passing the pump and supplying the lower floor by direct city pressure

35._____

36. Within a building, the piping material LEAST often used for water supply is

   A. galvanized iron   B. brass
   C. copper   D. cast iron

36._____

37. The purpose of a stop-and-waste valve is to

   A. drain a pipe when water flow is shut off
   B. prevent unnecessary use of water
   C. limit the pressure of water entering a fixture
   D. test the level of water in a boiler

37._____

38. One disadvantage in the use of a pneumatic tank for storage of water is that

   A. it is difficult to control the water pressure in this type tank
   B. this system cannot be used in conjunction with a gravity system
   C. only about 3/4 of the tank capacity can be used for water
   D. the system is limited to low buildings

38._____

39. A dry pipe sprinkler system would MOST likely be found in a building that

   A. is not heated   B. is low
   C. also has a standpipe   D. has two sources of supply

39._____

40. Of the following, the MAXIMUM design working pressure for a standard brass fitting is _____ psi.

   A. 50   B. 75   C. 100   D. 125

40._____

KEY (CORRECT ANSWERS)

1. C	11. D	21. A	31. C
2. B	12. C	22. A	32. B
3. A	13. A	23. D	33. D
4. D	14. D	24. A	34. A
5. D	15. C	25. B	35. B
6. D	16. A	26. D	36. D
7. D	17. B	27. B	37. A
8. B	18. B	28. D	38. C
9. B	19. D	29. A	39. A
10. C	20. C	30. B	40. D

TEST 2

DIRECTIONS: Each question or incomplete statement is followed by several suggested answers or completions. Select the one that BEST answers the question or completes the statement. *PRINT THE LETTER OF THE CORRECT ANSWER IN THE SPACE AT THE RIGHT.*

1. Electrolysis MOST often affects a water supply system by

    A. changing the taste of the water
    B. corroding the pipe
    C. creating a shock hazard
    D. clouding the water

    1._____

2. Assume that water drawn from a tap appears milky. The milky appearance then disappears when the water is allowed to stand.
   The gas that caused this milky appearance is MOST likely

    A. chlorine   B. fluorine   C. xenon   D. oxygen

    2._____

3. The law requires that where tubing is permitted for water supply, the joints MUST be

    A. silver soldered   B. soft soldered
    C. wiped   D. caulked

    3._____

4. An angle valve is a type of _____ valve.

    A. gate   B. globe
    C. compression   D. butterfly

    4._____

5. An inspector would MOST likely see a saddle fitting

    A. at a 4-way cross
    B. where a new connection has been added to an existing pipe line
    C. where the pressure of the supply is greater than city pressure
    D. at the outlet of a high pressure boiler

    5._____

6. Of the following, the one that is NOT a cause of continual running of water in a water closet flush tank is a

    A. punctured float
    B. rubber ball that does not seat
    C. broken trap seal tube
    D. worn valve seat

    6._____

7. In public areas, it is MOST desirable that a drinking fountain be so constructed that

    A. a high velocity spray comes out when the valve is opened
    B. water cannot drip back onto the nozzle
    C. the water valve will remain open without the user having to hold it
    D. the nozzle outlet be below the rim of the fountain

    7._____

37

8. Dirty water, caused by corrosion in pipes, will MOST likely appear in
    A. the hot water pipes first
    B. the cold water pipes first
    C. both hot and cold water pipes at about the same time
    D. either the hot or the cold water pipes first depending on the contamination in the water

9. While you are inspecting an apartment house for leaks, one of the tenants complains to you that she frequently gets hot water from the cold water faucet. This condition could result from improper installation of an appliance in another apartment.
    Of the following, the appliance or fixture that could MOST likely cause this problem is a
    A. dishwasher   B. kitchen sink
    C. clothes washing machine   D. bath tub

10. Of the following, the one that will NOT be likely to result in leaks in threaded pipe joints is
    A. pipe not reamed   B. threaded length too short
    C. lack of pipe dope   D. crossed threads

11. When a meter pit also contains a sewer trap, one of the requirements that MUST be met is that the pit must have a(n)
    A. air vent
    B. solid concrete cover
    C. removable steel ladder
    D. fixed name plate identifying the trap

12. When a booster pump is used on a water pressure booster system, the discharge end MUST be provided with a
    A. pressure regulator valve
    B. high pressure cut-off
    C. check valve
    D. vacuum breaker

13. A foot valve is generally found in the
    A. intake line of a boiler
    B. outlet line of a steam radiator
    C. bottom line of a tank
    D. suction line of a pump

14. There are two indicators used to determine the safety record of an agency. One is the *frequency of injury*; the other is the *severity of injury*.
    The *frequency of injury* is considered a better indicator of the safety record because
    A. blind chance has a greater effect on *severity* than on *frequency*
    B. it is easier to record *frequency* than *severity*
    C. workers will pay more attention to *frequency* than to *severity*
    D. it is more difficult to determine the *severity* than the *frequency*

15. It is frequently said that some people are *accident prone*. This term should be applied ONLY to those people who

   A. fail to respond to safety training
   B. have accidents when the cause of the accident cannot be determined
   C. lack the physical capacity for their job
   D. do not have the skill required to do a certain job

16. *Accidents frequently happen because a man "daydreams" on the job.*
    Of the following, the one that is CORRECT based on the previous sentence is:

   A. Accidents are most often caused by *daydreaming*
   B. The main cause of poor work is accidents
   C. A man who does not *daydream* is a good worker
   D. It is important for a man to pay attention to what he is doing

17. Accidents can be classified as caused either by *unsafe acts* or *unsafe conditions*.
    The one of the following that would be considered as *unsafe condition* is

   A. jumping over an obstruction on the floor
   B. poor lighting in a crowded cellar
   C. speeding in a motor vehicle
   D. use of the wrong tool for a job

18. One of the things an inspector should avoid doing is

   A. answering unimportant questions asked by the public
   B. talking to people he does not know
   C. blaming his supervisors for all the unpleasant orders the inspector must issue
   D. showing an interest in the public problems

19. An angry building owner complains loudly to you about the actions of the water use inspectors assigned to you.
    You should

   A. try to find excuses for your men's actions
   B. speak to him in the same tone of voice he is using
   C. insist that the actions of your men are correct
   D. try to answer his complaint quietly

20. In dealing with the general public, an inspector should remember that

   A. every person is an individual who may think for himself
   B. all people tend to think alike
   C. most people think alike
   D. it is best to change the public's way of thinking to what the department requires

21. An inspector is performing his job in the BEST manner when he

   A. continually checks with his senior inspector to make sure each inspection is being done properly
   B. knows enough to overlook minor violations that have a negligible effect on overall water use
   C. varies the Rules when he feels they do not meet the conditions of the job
   D. is careful and observant in his inspections

4 (#2)

22. The comma is used properly in which one of the following sentences?

    A. The plumber installed a, valve, meter, and by-pass in the cellar.
    B. The plumber installed a valve, meter, and by-pass, in the cellar.
    C. The plumber installed a valve, meter, and by-pass in the cellar.
    D. The plumber installed a valve, meter, and, by-pass, in the cellar.

23. A mistake was made in writing the following sentence:
    "An aproved water meter was installed because public water is being supplied to a business use."
    The mistake is that

    A. a word is misspelled
    B. the period should be placed after the quotation marks
    C. one of the words should start with a capital letter
    D. there should be a hyphen between two of the words

24. The following rule applies to all refrigeration systems heretofore installed.
    Heretofore, as used above, means MOST NEARLY

    A. to be   B. before this time
    C. in this location   D. improperly

25. The thought given in the sentence below is expressed BEST by:

    A. The meter was removed by a permit from this Department.
    B. The meter was removed with a permit from the Department.
    C. The meter was removed because of a permit from this Department.
    D. The meter was removed under authority of a permit from this Department.

26. An inspector makes a record of a meter reading on a *Meter Reading Sheet.*
    Of the following, the item of information that appears on this sheet is the

    A. size of tap
    B. area and height of building
    C. dial capacity
    D. type of business

27. A Water Use Inspector's Daily Route Slip differs from his Daily Summary Sheet in that the Summary Sheet indicates the

    A. number of different types of inspections made
    B. time each inspection was made
    C. number of inspections on hand that have not yet been made
    D. type of meter inspected

28. Meter records for a specific premises are filed in the office by

    A. street address   B. meter number
    C. block and lot   D. type of meter

29. When an inspector writes up a notice of leak and waste to be given to an owner, he also makes up an office copy.
The office copy differs from the inspector's notice to the owner in that the office copy

   A. does not indicate *Total Fixtures in Building*
   B. has provision for entering the inspector's report of reinspection of premises
   C. shows the scale of fines for wasting water
   D. lists the conditions under which the notice should be given the owner

30. An important characteristic of a good supervisor is his ability to

   A. be a stern disciplinarian
   B. put off the settling of grievances
   C. solve problems
   D. find fault in individuals

31. At the time you hand out a job assignment, an inspector feels that he cannot complete the job within the time limit you have given him.
You would expect the inspector FIRST to

   A. make as many inspections as possible and then report to you
   B. compare his workload to that of the other inspectors
   C. complete the work by putting in overtime before notifying you of the problem
   D. request assistance in doing the work

32. A new inspector will BEST obtain the respect of the men assigned to him if he

   A. makes decisions rapidly and sticks to them, regardless of whether they are right or wrong
   B. makes decisions rapidly and then changes them just as rapidly if the decisions are wrong
   C. does not make any decisions unless he is absolutely sure that they are right
   D. makes his decisions after considering carefully all available information

33. A newly appointed inspector is operating at a level of performance below that of the other employees.
In this situation, a supervisor should FIRST

   A. lower the acceptable standard for the new inspector
   B. find out why the new inspector cannot do as well as the others
   C. advise the new inspector he will be dropped from the payroll at the end of the probationary period
   D. assign another new inspector to assist the first inspector

34. Assume that you have to instruct a new man on a specific departmental operation. The new man seems unsure of what you have said.
Of the following, the BEST way for you to determine whether the man has understood you is to

   A. have the man explain the operation to you in his own words
   B. repeat your explanation to him slowly
   C. repeat your explanation to him, using simpler wording
   D. emphasize the important parts of the operation to him

35. An inspector realizes that he has taken an instantaneous dislike to a new inspector assigned to him.
The BEST course of action to take in this case is to

    A. be especially observant of the new inspector's actions
    B. request that the new inspector be reassigned
    C. make a special effort to be fair to the new inspector
    D. ask to be transferred himself

36. A supervisor gives detailed instructions to his men as to how a certain type of job is to be done.
One advantage of this practice is that this will

    A. result in a more flexible operation
    B. standardize operations
    C. encourage new men to learn
    D. encourage initiative in the men

37. Of the following, the one that would MOST likely be the result of poor planning is

    A. omissions are discovered after the work is completed
    B. during the course of normal inspection a meter is found to be inaccessible
    C. an inspector completes his assignments for that day ahead of schedule
    D. a problem arises during an inspection and prevents an inspector from completing his day's assignments

38. Of the following, the BEST way for a supervisor to maintain good employee morale is for the supervisor to

    A. avoid correcting the employee when he makes mistakes
    B. continually praise the employee's work even when it is of average quality
    C. show that he is willing to assist in solving the employee's problems
    D. accept the employee's excuses for failure even though the excuses are not valid

39. A supervisor takes time to explain to his men why a departmental order has been issued.
This practice is

    A. *good*, mainly because without this explanation the men will not be able to carry out the order
    B. *bad*, mainly because time will be wasted for no useful purpose
    C. *good*, because understanding the reasons behind an order will lead to more effective carrying out of the order
    D. *bad*, because men will then question every order that they receive

40. Some degree of hazard is associated with every form of activity; therefore, the highest degree of accident elimination can be achieved only by careful, painstaking attention to safety in every form of activity.
According to the above statement,

    A. all accidents can be eliminated by being careful and attentive
    B. most accidents occur because of a combination of physical condition and human error
    C. accidents can occur in any job
    D. most types of work injuries cannot be prevented

KEY (CORRECT ANSWERS)

1.	B	11.	A	21.	D	31.	D
2.	D	12.	C	22.	C	32.	D
3.	A	13.	D	23.	A	33.	B
4.	B	14.	A	24.	B	34.	A
5.	B	15.	A	25.	D	35.	C
6.	C	16.	D	26.	C	36.	B
7.	B	17.	B	27.	A	37.	A
8.	A	18.	C	28.	C	38.	C
9.	C	19.	D	29.	B	39.	C
10.	A	20.	A	30.	C	40.	C

EXAMINATION SECTION
TEST 1

DIRECTIONS: Each question or incomplete statement is followed by several suggested answers or completions. Select the one that BEST answers the question or completes the statement. *PRINT THE LETTER OF THE CORRECT ANSWER IN THE SPACE AT THE RIGHT.*

1. While inspecting water meters in a large office building, an inspector notices some structural beams sagging in what appears to be a dangerous manner.
   Of the following, the inspector should

   A. take no action since it is the Building Department that has jurisdiction over building structures
   B. advise the person in charge of the building to consult the Building Department
   C. notify the Police Department so that the building can be evacuated
   D. report his observation to his superior so that the Building Department can be notified

   1.____

2. Firemen sometimes find it necessary to draft salt water for use on fires. However, their departmental regulations forbid the use of salt water in any standpipe or sprinkler system.
   The MAIN reason for this prohibition is that salt water may

   A. corrode the pipes
   B. contaminate the domestic water supply
   C. cause more water damage than fresh water
   D. react chemically with some unknown substances in the building

   2.____

3. An inspector is investigating a complaint that a water meter is not operating properly. While making his examination in the basement of the building, he notices that one of the water taps is leaking.
   Of the following, the BEST course for him to follow is to

   A. recommend to his superior that another inspector be sent to the building to inspect the water taps
   B. change the washer in the tap's stem
   C. serve notice on the person in charge to correct the condition
   D. shut off the water supply to that tap

   3.____

4. An inspector who is inspecting meters finds a large dog with a menacing bark barring his way to meters in the basement of a building.
   In this situation, the BEST course of action for the inspector to follow is to

   A. try to locate the superintendent of the building
   B. make the inspection, ignoring the dog who probably will not bite
   C. leave without making the inspection and return on some other day
   D. notify the police and request that they remove the dog so that the inspection can be made

   4.____

5. Consumers are advised to turn off the water supply to their houses whenever they close the houses for any period of time.
   The MAIN reason for this practice is to prevent

   5.____

45

A. loss of water pressure in the event of a major fire in the area
B. build-up of excessive pressure in the pipes in the event that there is malfunctioning of the pumping system
C. occurrence of leaks during the family's absence
D. corrosion of the plumbing system during the period of disuse

6. The MAIN objection to the practice of leaving faucets open on cold nights in order to prevent freezing of water pipes is that

A. water is wasted
B. pipes will freeze even with open faucets
C. unnecessary strain is placed on the plumbing system
D. water pressure is lowered in the system

7. A permit for a tap for unmetered water will be issued only on *pre-payment* of all charges for water to be used.
The word *pre-payment*, as used above, means

A. promise of payment
B. payment in advance
C. payment as water is used
D. monthly payment

8. Upon application, the department will *endeavor* to locate a service pipe by means of an electrical indicator.
The word *endeavor*, as used above, means

A. try B. help C. assist D. explore

9. It shall be unlawful for any person to operate a fire hydrant without *previous* permission from the department.
The word *previous*, as used above, means

A. written B. oral
C. prior D. provisional

10. All persons must *comply* with the rules and regulations.
The word *comply*, as used above, means

A. agree B. coincide
C. work carefully D. act in accord

11. No unauthorized person shall *tamper with* a water supply valve.
The words *tamper with*, as used above, mean

A. open B. operate C. alter D. shut

12. The use of water is permitted subject to such conditions as the department may consider *reasonable*.
The word *reasonable*, as used above, means

A. necessary B. inexpensive
C. fair D. desirable

13. An owner must *engage* a licensed plumber.
    The word *engage,* as used above, means

    A. hire B. pay C. contact D. inform

14. The charges for a tap are usually for the *furnishing,* delivering, and installing of the tap.
    The word *furnishing*, as used above, means

    A. preparing B. manufacturing
    C. finishing D. supplying

15. The investigator attempted to *ascertain* the facts.
    As used in this sentence, the word *ascertain* means MOST NEARLY

    A. disprove B. find out
    C. go beyond D. explain

16. The speaker *commenced* the lecture with an anecdote.
    As used in this sentence, the word *commenced* means MOST NEARLY

    A. concluded B. illustrated
    C. enlivened D. started

17. The use of a hydrant may be *authorized* for construction purposes.
    The word *authorized,* as used above, means

    A. possible B. permitted C. intended D. stopped

Questions 18-20.

DIRECTIONS: Questions 18 through 20 shall be answered in accordance with the paragraph below.

A connection for commercial, purposes may be made from a metered fire or sprinkler line of 4 inches or larger in diameter, provided a meter is installed on the commercial branch line. Such connection shall be taken from the inlet side of the fire meter control valve, and the method of connection shall be subject to the approval of the department. On a 4-inch fire line, the connection shall not exceed 1 1/2 inches in diameter. On a fire line 6 inches or larger in diameter, the size of the connection shall not exceed 2 inches. Fire lines shall not be cross-connected with any system of piping within the building.

18. According to the above paragraph, a connection for commercial purposes may be made to a metered sprinkler line provided that the diameter of the sprinkler line is AT LEAST

    A. 1 1/2" B. 2" C. 4" D. 6"

19. According to the above paragraph, the connection for commercial purposes is taken from the

    A. inlet side of the main control valve
    B. outlet side of the wet connection
    C. inlet side of the fire meter control valve
    D. outlet side of the Siamese

4 (#1)

20. According to the above paragraph, the MAXIMUM size permitted for the connection for commercial purposes depends on the

   A. location of the fire meter valve
   B. use to which the commercial line is to be put
   C. method of connection to the sprinkler line
   D. size of the sprinkler line

20.____

Questions 21-22.

DIRECTIONS: Questions 21 and 22 are to be answered in accordance with the paragraph below.

Meters shall be set or reset so that they may be easily examined and read. In all premises where the supply of water is to be fully metered, the meter shall be set within three feet of the building or vault wall at point of entry of service pipe. The service pipe between meter control valve and meter shall be kept exposed. When a building is situated back of the building line or conditions exist in a building that prevent the setting of the meter at a point of entry, meter may be set outside of the building in a proper watertight and frost-proof pit or meter box, or at other location approved by the Deputy Commissioner, Assistant to Commissioner, or the Chief Inspector.

21. According to the above paragraph, a meter should be set

   A. at a point in the building convenient to the owner
   B. within 3 feet of the building wall
   C. in back of the building
   D. where the district inspector thinks is best

21.____

22. According to the above paragraph, one of the conditions imposed when a meter is permitted to be installed outside of a building is that the meter must be installed

   A. between the service pipe and the meter control valve
   B. within 3 feet of the point of entry of the service pipe
   C. in a watertight enclosure
   D. above ground in a frost-proof box

22.____

Questions 23-26.

DIRECTIONS: Questions 23 through 26 are to be answered in accordance with the following paragraphs.

No individual or collective air conditioning system installed on any premises for a single consumer shall be permitted to waste annually more than the equivalent of a continuous flow of five gallons of city water per minute.

All individual or collective air conditioning systems installed on any premises for a single consumer using city water annually in excess of the equivalent of five gallons per minute shall be equipped with a water conserving device such as economizer, evaporative condenser, water cooling tower or other similar apparatus, which device shall not consume for make-up purposes in excess of 15% of the consumption that would normally be used without such device.

Any individual or collective group of such units installed on any premises for a single consumer with a rated capacity of 25 tons or more, or water consumption of 50 gallons or more per minute, shall be equipped, where required by the department, with a water meter to separately register the consumption of such unit or groups of units.

This rule shall also apply to all air conditioning equipment now in service.

23. The rules described in the above paragraphs apply 23.____

    A. *only* to new installations of air conditioning equipment
    B. *only* to air conditioning systems which waste more than 5 gallons of city water per minute
    C. *only* to hew installations of air conditioning equipment which waste more than 5 gallons of city water per minute
    D. to all air conditioning systems, whether existing ones or new installations

24. According to the above paragraphs, one of the acceptable methods of reducing wasting of water in an air conditioning system is by means of a 24.____

    A. cooling tower   B. water meter
    C. check valve   D. collective system

25. According to the above paragraphs, the department may require that an air conditioning system have a separate water meter when the system 25.____

    A. wastes more than 5 gallons of city water per minute
    B. uses more than 15% make-up water
    C. is equipped with an economizer
    D. has a rated capacity of 25 tons or more

26. According to the above paragraphs, the MAXIMUM quantity of make-up water permitted where an air conditioning system uses 50 gallons of water per minute is _____ gal./min. 26.____

    A. 7   B. 7 1/2   C. 8   D. 8 1/2

Questions 27-28.

DIRECTIONS: Questions 27 and 28 are to be answered in accordance with the paragraph below.

Where flushometers, suction tanks, other fixtures or piping are equipped with quick closing valves and are supplied by direct street pressure in excess of 70 pounds, an air chamber of an approved type shall be installed within two feet of the house control valve or meter in the service near the point of entry. Where water hammer conditions exist in any installation, regardless of the pressure obtaining, an air chamber of an approved type shall be installed where and as directed by the Chief Inspector or Engineer.

27. According to the above paragraph, air chambers are required when or wherever 27.____

    A. there are flushometers
    B. piping is supplied at a direct street pressure in excess of 70 lbs. per square inch
    C. a quick closing valve is used
    D. water hammer can occur in any piping

28. According to the above paragraph, air chambers should be installed   28.____

   A. within two feet of the house control valve or meter
   B. in a water system regardless of operating pressure
   C. on the fixture side of the quick closing valve
   D. on the suction side of the service meter

Questions 29-32.

DIRECTIONS: Questions 29 through 32, inclusive, refer to the paragraphs, tables, and building floor plans shown below.

The annual frontage rents on premises wholly or partly unmetered shall be as follows:

Front Width of Building	One Story Height	Front Width of Building	One Story Height
16 ft. and under	$ 6.00	Over 22 1/2 ft. -25 ft.	$12.00
Over 16 ft. -18 ft.	7.50	Over 25 ft. -20 ft.	15.00
Over 18 ft. -20 ft.	9.00	Over 30 ft. -37 1/2 ft.	18.00
Over 20 ft. -22 1/2 ft.	10.50	Over 37 1/2 ft. -50 ft.	21.00

For each additional story, $1.50 per annum shall be added; and for each additional ten (10) feet or part thereof above fifty feet in front width of building, $3.00 shall be added.

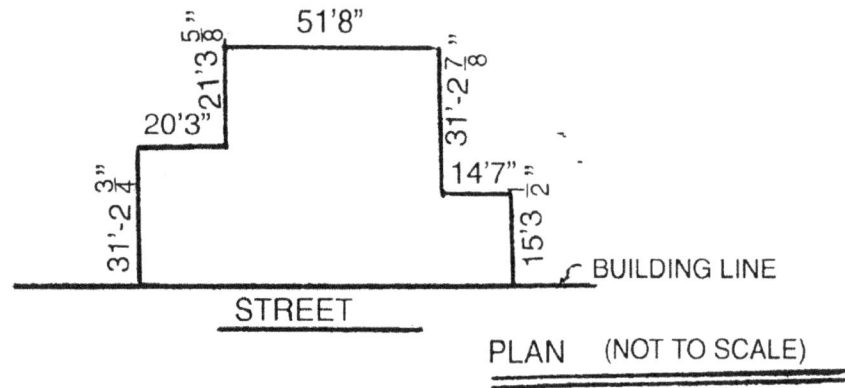

PLAN   (NOT TO SCALE)

29. The front width of this building is   29.____

   A. 85'11"   B. 86'0"   C. 86'1"   D. 86'2"

30. The MAXIMUM depth of the above building is   30.____

   A. 51'5 3/4"   B. 52'5"   C. 52'6 3/8"   D. 66'7 3/8"

31. If the above building is only one story high, the frontage rent is   31.____

   A. $30.00   B. $31.50   C. $33.00   D. $34.50

32. If the above building is three stories high, the frontage rent is   32.____

   A. $31.50   B. $33.00   C. $34.50   D. $36.00

33. Of the following materials, the one which is NOT used in the city for supplying domestic water in a plumbing system is 33._____

   A. red brass
   B. yellow brass
   C. plastic
   D. galvanized cast iron

34. A simple pressure gauge installed on a water line is USUALLY used to _____ water pressure. 34._____

   A. relieve excessive
   B. control the
   C. measure the
   D. decrease the

35. A *standpipe system* is generally used to supply water to the 35._____

   A. domestic water system
   B. wet sprinkler system
   C. fire hose
   D. house tank

KEY (CORRECT ANSWERS)

1.	D	16.	D
2.	B	17.	B
3.	C	18.	C
4.	A	19.	C
5.	C	20.	D
6.	A	21.	B
7.	B	22.	C
8.	A	23.	D
9.	C	24.	A
10.	D	25.	D
11.	C	26.	B
12.	C	27.	D
13.	A	28.	A
14.	D	29.	B
15.	B	30.	C

31. C
32. D
33. C
34. C
35. C

TEST 2

DIRECTIONS: Each question or incomplete statement is followed by several suggested answers or completions. Select the one that BEST answers the question or completes the statement. *PRINT THE LETTER OF THE CORRECT ANSWER IN THE SPACE AT THE RIGHT.*

Questions 1-4.

DIRECTIONS: Questions 1 through 4, inclusive, refer to the sketches of the floor plan of 3 buildings shown below.

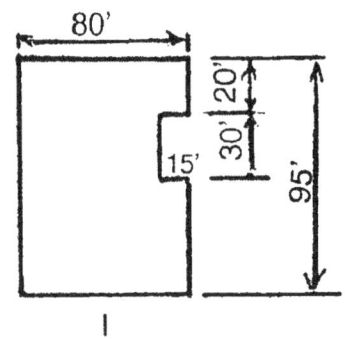
I

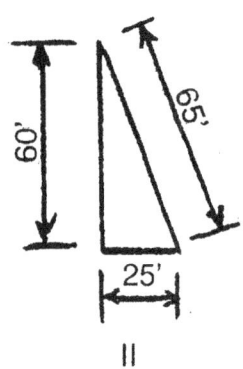
II

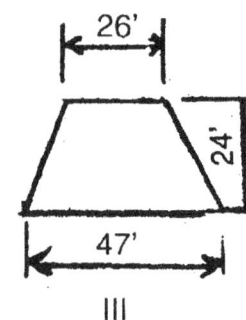
III

Sketches not to scale

1. The area in square feet of each floor of building #I is MOST NEARLY　　　　1.____
   A. 7150　　　　B. 7600　　　　C. 8050　　　　D. 8500

2. The area in square feet of each floor of building #II is MOST NEARLY　　　　2.____
   A. 750　　　　B. 817　　　　C. 1500　　　　D. 1625

3. The area in square feet of each floor of building #III is MOST NEARLY　　　　3.____
   A. 504　　　　B. 876　　　　C. 1460　　　　D. 1756

4. The area of building #I is MOST NEARLY _____ times that of building #III.　　　　4.____
   A. 5　　　　B. 6　　　　C. 7　　　　D. 8

5. The plumbing term *furred-in* generally means that the plumbing pipes are

    A. hidden
    B. exposed
    C. insulated
    D. made watertight

Questions 6-9.

DIRECTIONS: Questions 6 through 9, inclusive, refer to the diagram of the dials of a water meter shown below.

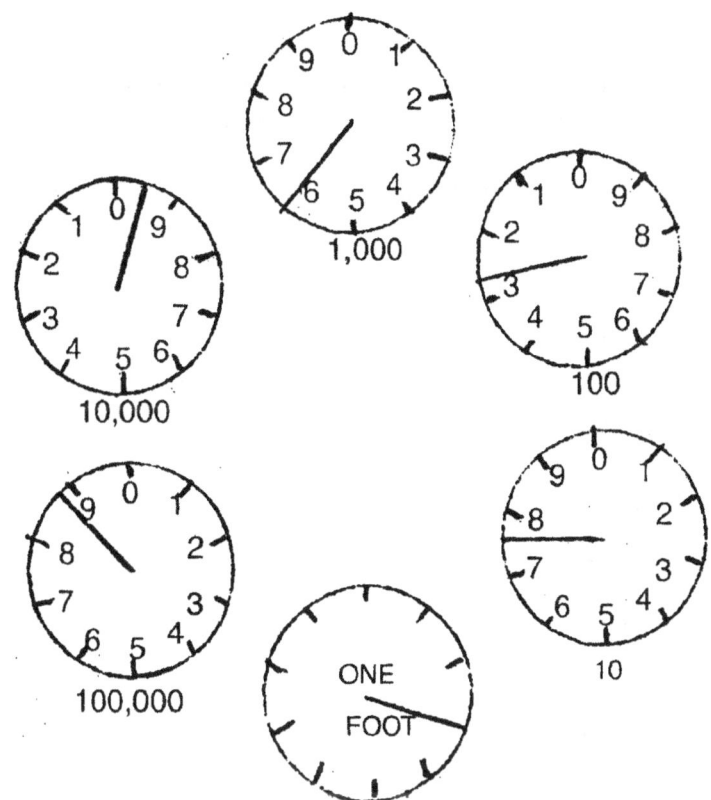

6. The CORRECT reading of the meter, in cubic feet, is

    A. 72698   B. 89627   C. 90637   D. 80637

7. For each complete revolution of the hand on the dial marked 10,000, the hand on the dial marked 10 revolves _____ times.

    A. 3   B. 20   C. 300   D. 1,000

8. The statement MOST NEARLY CORRECT is that the hands on _____ rotate in a _____ direction.

    A. all the dials; clockwise
    B. all the dials; counterclockwise
    C. the dials marked 10, 1,000, and 100,000; clockwise
    D. the dials marked 10, 1,000, and 100,000; counterclockwise

9. If the hand on the 1000 dial was exactly on the number 7, and then moved to the number 8, the hand on the 100 dial would move

   A. one space clockwise
   B. completely around the dial and stop in the same place it was originally
   C. one space counterclockwise
   D. one or more spaces, depending on the water flow

10. The MAIN purpose of a house roof tank for plumbing fixtures in a building is to

    A. conserve usage of water
    B. provide a storage place when the water is not in demand
    C. insure necessary water pressure at the plumbing fixtures
    D. provide a means of chemically treating the water

11. A short piece of straight 1/2" diameter pipe 2" long and having male threads at both ends is USUALLY called a

    A. coupling   B. union   C. nipple   D. stud

12. A hypochlorite solution is USUALLY used for

    A. disinfecting water tanks
    B. soldering
    C. preventing rust formation in pipes
    D. cleaning water meters

13. The size of a water meter is USUALLY governed by the

    A. diameter of the service pipe
    B. diameter of the tap
    C. available space where installed
    D. pressure in the main

14. An automatic water regulating valve is a valve that is

    A. free flowing   B. one way
    C. self-regulating   D. a control valve

15. The MINIMUM diameter, in inches, of water supply branches made of ferrous material, connected to fixtures other than those connected to flush valves is

    A. 3/8"   B. 1/2"   C. 5/8"   D. 3/4"

16. The type of water meter that operates without moving parts is GENERALLY known as a _____ meter.

    A. compound   B. venturi   C. turbine   D. disc

17. A water service pipe is USUALLY laid in a straight line at right angles to the street main in order to

    A. increase frictional losses
    B. make rodding easier
    C. shorten the run of pipe
    D. reduce the amount of excavation

18. The size of a water service pipe for commercial and industrial use is USUALLY determined on the basis of the

    A. building floor area
    B. water pressure
    C. number of floors in a building
    D. water demand load

19. The MINIMUM size of service pipe permitted for commercial and industrial use is

    A. 3/4"   B. 1"   C. 1 1/4"   D. 1 1/2"

20. The size of a corporation cock should be

    A. one size smaller than the size of service pipe
    B. one size larger than the size of service pipe
    C. equal to the size of service pipe
    D. not greater than 3/4"

21. A *wet connection* is made when the water in the main is

    A. shut off   B. under pressure
    C. by-passed   D. leaking

22. A corporation cock is used MAINLY for

    A. shutting off the water B. tap connections
    C. regulating the flow   D. wet connections

23. The size of the hole permitted in the water main for a tap connection depends upon the

    A. size of the main
    B. pressure in the main
    C. pipe material of the main
    D. spacing of the taps

24. A water service pipe is defined as that portion of the water pipe extending from the public main to the

    A. curb valve and box
    B. furthest fixture
    C. building line
    D. main house control valve

25. The type of water meter, 3" or larger, that is USUALLY used where there is a fluctuating flow of water or a pressure feed water system is called a _____ meter.

    A. displacement   B. current
    C. compound   D. fire-service

26. A water meter is a device that is used to measure the water

    A. pressure   B. velocity   C. consumed   D. hardness

27. A pressure of 25 psi in the street main may be sufficient to supply water to a building that is NOT more than _____ feet high.

    A. 40   B. 60   C. 80   D. 100

28. The MINIMUM distance that a vacuum breaker should be set, above the floor level rim of a fixture, is

    A. 1" B. 2" C. 3" D. 4"

29. The one of the following types of buildings which does NOT require the installation of a water meter is a

    A. public library
    B. hotel
    C. factory
    D. canning plant

30. The city is NOT required to maintain a minimum water pressure in a premise other than that required to deliver water to the

    A. top floor fixture
    B. roof tank
    C. standpipe system (gravity)
    D. basement

31. After a tap has been inserted in a water main and the service pipe installed, the type of backfill around and one foot over the main and service should be

    A. clean earth
    B. gravel
    C. asphalt concrete
    D. tanbark

32. According to the city code, water supply lines to hot water boilers, steam boilers, or similar equipment MUST be equipped with a

    A. vacuum breaker
    B. check valve
    C. pressure reducing valve
    D. compound gauge

33. The one of the following chemicals which is used to soften water is

    A. calcium carbonate
    B. slaked lime
    C. magnesium sulphate
    D. calcium chloride

34. A sounding rod is used to

    A. locate leaks in buried water pipes
    B. locate the trouble in a noisy meter
    C. determine the cause of pipe vibration
    D. locate water hammer in a pipe line

35. The purpose of a float-controlled valve used in a water-closet flush tank is to maintain a

    A. continuous water supply to the tank
    B. constant water level in the tank
    C. back pressure in the water line
    D. quiet water feed

KEY (CORRECT ANSWERS)

1.	A	16.	B
2.	A	17.	B
3.	B	18.	D
4.	D	19.	B
5.	A	20.	A
6.	B	21.	B
7.	D	22.	D
8.	C	23.	A
9.	B	24.	D
10.	C	25.	C
11.	C	26.	C
12.	A	27.	A
13.	B	28.	D
14.	C	29.	A
15.	B	30.	D

31. A
32. B
33. B
34. A
35. B

EXAMINATION SECTION
TEST 1

DIRECTIONS: Each question or incomplete statement is followed by several suggested answers or completions. Select the one that BEST answers the question or completes the statement. *PRINT THE LETTER OF THE CORRECT ANSWER IN THE SPACE AT THE RIGHT.*

1. An inspector is offered a box of cigars for Christmas by the owner of several small commercial buildings.
   Of the following, the BEST course for the inspector to take is to

   A. refuse the gift and warn the owner about the penalties for attempting to bribe an inspector
   B. accept the gift and send it to the local veterans' hospital
   C. refuse the gift but soothe the owner's feelings by saying that he doesn't smoke
   D. refuse the gift and explain that the department's regulations prohibit acceptance of any gifts

2. The MAIN reason for placing a seal on a water meter is to

   A. keep a record of the dates on which the meter was inspected
   B. prevent contamination of water
   C. indicate tampering with the meter
   D. show that it is an approved meter

3. An inspector who is reading a meter in the cellar of an apartment house, is approached by a man who appears to be intoxicated. The man makes abusive remarks about government employees, calling them lazy and dishonest.
   In this situation, the inspector should

   A. attempt to persuade the man that he is mistaken in his opinions
   B. call for a policeman to have the man arrested for abusing a government employee in the performance of his duty
   C. make his readings without answering the man
   D. ask the man for proof of his charges

4. While reading a water meter, an inspector was engaged in conversation by a talkative woman. When the inspector completed his reading, the woman was still talking, and, obviously, had much more to say. The inspector skillfully ended the conversation, politely said goodbye, and left.
   The inspector's method of handing this situation was

   A. *proper;* inspectors should never talk to the public except about business
   B. *not proper;* the inspector should not have permitted the woman to start the conversation in the first place
   C. *proper;* inspectors should not waste time in idle conversation
   D. *not proper;* the inspector should have waited until the woman was finished in order to create good will for the department

5. An inspector, checking the seals on a water meter in the basement of an apartment house, is approached by a man who asks what he is doing. The inspector tells the man that he is from the department of water supply, gas and electricity and that he is checking the meter. The man then demands to see his credentials.
The inspector should

   A. show his identification card to the man
   B. ignore the man and continue his work
   C. find out whether the man is a tenant or superintendent of the building
   D. tell the man that he should call the department of water supply, gas and electricity if he is not satisfied with the explanation

6. While reading a meter, an inspector notices some defective plumbing and advises the owner of the condition. The owner offers the job to the inspector, to be done on his free time. In this situation, the inspector should

   A. agree to do the work if he has the spare time and wants the additional money
   B. refuse to do the work, explaining that it would be a violation of the department's policy
   C. refuse the work but recommend a reliable plumber
   D. advise the owner how he could do the work himself

7. An inspector, while reading the water meter in a restaurant, is invited by the owner to have lunch "on the house."
The inspector should

   A. accept the invitation but select the cheapest meal on the menu
   B. refuse the invitation but thank the owner for the offer
   C. accept the invitation but refuse any alcoholic beverages
   D. refuse the invitation and tell the owner that he can afford to pay for his meals

8. *Conservation* of the water supply is a major goal of the department.
The word *conservation* as used in this sentence means, most nearly,

   A. estimating   B. increasing   C. preserving   D. purifying

9. *Consumers* should inspect their meters frequently to guard against leaks.
The word *consumers* as used in this sentence means, most nearly,

   A. citizens   B. owners   C. producers   D. users

10. The wire was connected to the *adjacent* terminal.
The word *adjacent* as used in this sentence means, most nearly,

    A. out of order   B. metallic   C. nearby   D. negative

11. Some of the equipment supplied to the inspector was *defective*.
The word *defective* as used in this sentence means, most nearly,

    A. expensive   B. faulty   C. old   D. unnecessary

12. The inspector was told to use *discretion* in dealing with the public.
The word *discretion* as used in this sentence means, most nearly,

    A. courtesy   B. firmness   C. judgment   D. persuasion

13. It is unlawful to *demolish* any building without first obtaining a permit. 13._____
    The word *demolish* as used in this sentence means, most nearly,

    A. build
    B. make alterations in
    C. occupy
    D. tear down

14. The clerk *rendered* an account of the cash received. 14._____
    The word *rendered* as used in this sentence means, most nearly,

    A. concealed   B. corrected   C. forged   D. gave

15. The permit was *revoked* by the department. 15._____
    The word *revoked* as used in this sentence means, most nearly,

    A. approved   B. cancelled   C. renewed   D. reviewed

16. The *incident* received much attention in the newspapers. 16._____
    The word *incident* as used in this sentence means, most nearly,

    A. campaign   B. crime   C. event   D. merger

17. The *modification* of the procedure was approved by the supervisor. 17._____
    The word *modification* as used in this sentence means, most nearly,

    A. change   B. interpretation   C. repeal   D. termination

Questions 18-21.

DIRECTIONS: Questions 18 to 21, inclusive, are to be answered in accordance with the information given in the following paragraphs:

Air conditioning units requiring a minimum rate of flow of water in excess of one-half (1/2) gallon per minute shall be metered.

Air conditioning equipment with a refrigeration unit which has a definite rate of capacity in tons or fractions thereof, the charge will be at the rate of $30 per annum per ton capacity from the date installed to the date when the supply is metered. Such units, when equipped with an approved water-conserving device, shall be charged at the rate of $4.50 per annum per ton capacity from the date installed to the date when the supply is metered.

18. A man who was in the market for air conditioning equipment was considering three different units. 18._____
    Unit 1 required a flow of 28 gallons of water per hour; unit 2 required 30 gallons of water per hour; unit 3 required 32 gallons of water per hour.
    The man asked the salesman which units would require the installation of a water meter. According to the above passage, the salesman *should answer:*

    A. all three units require meters
    B. units 2 and 3 require meters
    C. unit 3 only requires a meter
    D. none of the units require a meter

19. Suppose that air conditioning equipment with a refrigeration unit of 10 tons was put in operation on October 1, and, in the following year, on July 1, a meter was installed. According to the above passage, the charge for this period would be

    A. twice the annual rate
    B. equal to the annual rate
    C. three-fourths the annual rate
    D. one-fourth the annual rate

20. The charge for air conditioning equipment which has no refrigeration unit

    A. is $30 per year
    B. is $25.50 per year
    C. is $4.50 per year
    D. cannot be determined from the above passage

21. The charge for air conditioning equipment with a seven-ton refrigeration unit equipped with an approved water-conserving device

    A. is $4.50 per year
    B. is $25.50 per year
    C. is $31.50 per year
    D. cannot be determined from the above passage

Questions 22-27.

DIRECTIONS: Questions 22 to 27, inclusive, relate to the following paragraph:

The city makes unremitting efforts to keep the water free from pollution. An inspectional force under a sanitary expert is engaged in patrolling the watersheds to see that the department's sanitary regulations are observed. Samples taken daily from various points in the water supply system are examined and analyzed at the three laboratories maintained by the department. All water before delivery to the distribution mains is treated with chlorine to destroy bacteria. In addition, some water is aerated to free it from gases and in some cases from microscopic organisms. Generally, microscopic organisms which develop in the reservoirs and at times impart an unpleasant taste and odor to the water, though in no sense harmful to health, are destroyed by treatment with copper sulfate and by chlorine dosage. None of the supplies is filtered, but the quality of the water supplied by the city is excellent for all purposes, and it is clear and wholesome.

22. According to the above paragraph, microscopic organisms are removed from the water supplied to the city by means of

    A. chlorine alone
    B. chlorine, aeration, and filtration
    C. chlorine, aeration, fultration, and sampling
    D. copper sulfate, chlorine, and aeration

23. Microscopic organisms in the water supply *generally* are

    A. a health menace
    B. impossible to detect
    C. not harmful to health
    D. not destroyed in the water

24. The MAIN function of the inspectional force, as described in the above paragraph, is to

    A. take samples of water for analysis
    B. enforce sanitary regulations
    C. add chlorine to the water supply
    D. inspect water-use meters

25. According to the above paragraph, chlorine is added to water before entering the

    A. watersheds
    B. reservoirs
    C. distribution mains
    D. run-off areas

26. Of the following suggested headings or titles for the above paragraph, the one that BEST tells what the paragraph is about is:

    A. QUALITY OF WATER
    B. CHLORINATION OF WATER
    C. TESTING OF WATER
    D. BACTERIA IN WATER

27. The *most likely* reason for taking samples of water for examination and analysis from various points in the water supply system is:

    A. The testing points are convenient to the department's laboratories
    B. Water from one part of the system may be made undrink-able by a local condition
    C. The samples can be distributed equally among the three laboratories
    D. The hardness or softness of water varies from place to place

Questions 28-30.

DIRECTIONS: Questions 28 to 30 inclusive, are to be answered in accordance with the information given in the paragraph below.

A building measuring 200" x 100' at the street is set back 20' on all sides at the 15th floor, and an additional 10' on all sides at the 30th floor. The building is 35 stories high.

28. The floor area of the 16th floor is, most nearly, _____ sq. ft.

    A. 20,000   B. 14,400   C. 9,600   D. 7,500

29. The floor area of the 35th floor is, most nearly, _____ sq. ft.

    A. 20,000   B. 13,900   C. 7,500   D. 5,600

30. The floor area of the 16th floor, compared to the floor area of the 2nd floor, is, most nearly, _____ as much.

    A. three-fourths (3/4)
    B. two-thirds (2/3)
    C. one-half (1/2)
    D. four-tenths (4/10)

31. On test, a meter registered one cubic foot for each 1 1/3 cubic feet of water that passed through it.
    If the meter had a reading of 1200 cubic feet, we may conclude that the *correct* amount should be _____ cubic ft.

    A. 800   B. 900   C. 1500   D. 1600

32. A water use meter reads 87,463 cubic feet.
    If the previous reading was 17,377 cubic feet, and the rate charged is 15 cents per 100 cubic feet, the bill for water use during this period is about

    A. $45.00   B. $65.00   C. $85.00   D. $105.00

Questions 33-35.

DIRECTIONS: Questions 33 to 35, inclusive, relate to the diagram of a meter on the following page.

33. The CORRECT reading of the meter which appears on page 6, is, in cubic feet, 33._____

    A. 198,277   B. 108,383   C. 99,388   D. 9,827

34. In the operation of the meter which appears on page 6, the rotation of the indicator on the dial marked ONE 34._____

    A. is in a clockwise direction
    B. is in a counter-clockwise direction
    C. is first in a clockwise, then in a counter-clockwise direction
    D. cannot be determined from the diagram

35. The *largest* quantity that can be recorded by the meter below is, in cubic feet, 35._____

    A. 10,000,000   B. 1,000,000   C. 100,000   D. 10,000

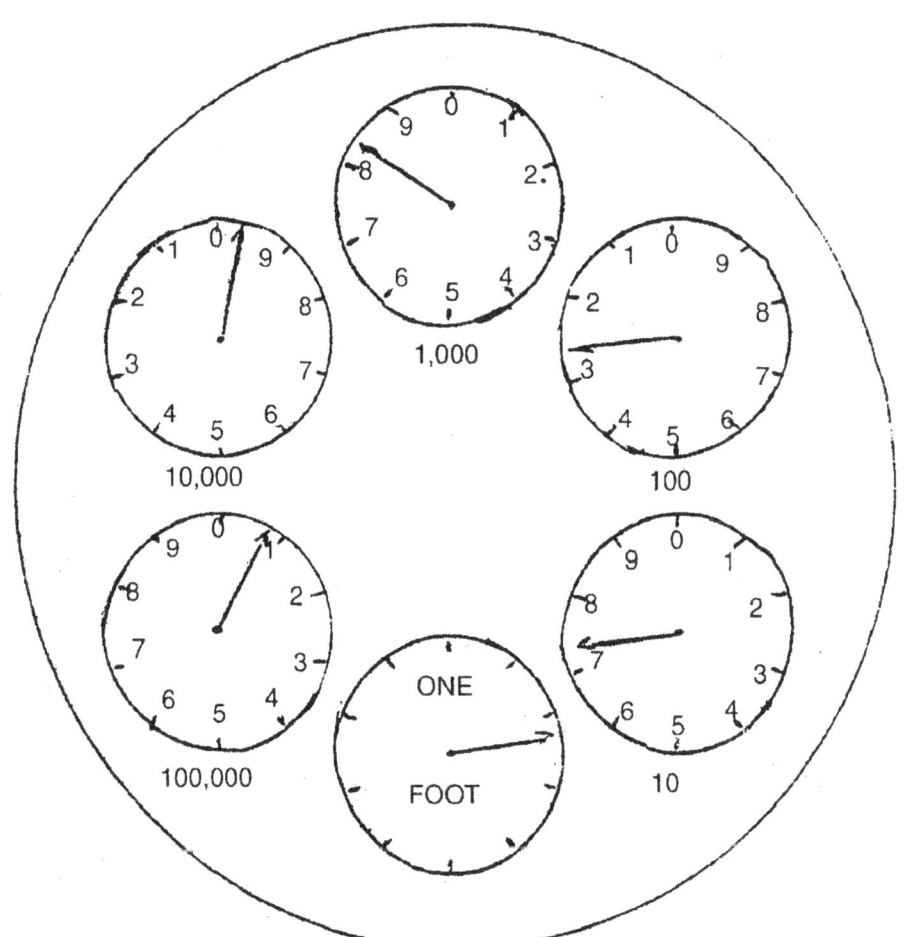

36. A leaking faucet caused the loss of .1 of a cubic foot of water every hour. The meter reading for April was 4,580 cubic feet.
    The amount of water lost through the faucet in that month was about _____. ft.   36._____

    A. 45.8   B. 72.0   C. 74.4   D. 458.0

37. Water is flowing into a cylindrical tank 10 feet high with a diameter of 6 feet.   37._____
    If the tank is filled in 56 minutes, the rate at which the water is entering the tank is about _____ cubic feet per minute.

    A. 2   B. 5   C. 8   D. 11

Questions 38-40.

DIRECTIONS: Questions 38 to 40, inclusive, relate to the diagrams immediately below. These diagrams represent the outline of the floor plans of 3 buildings.

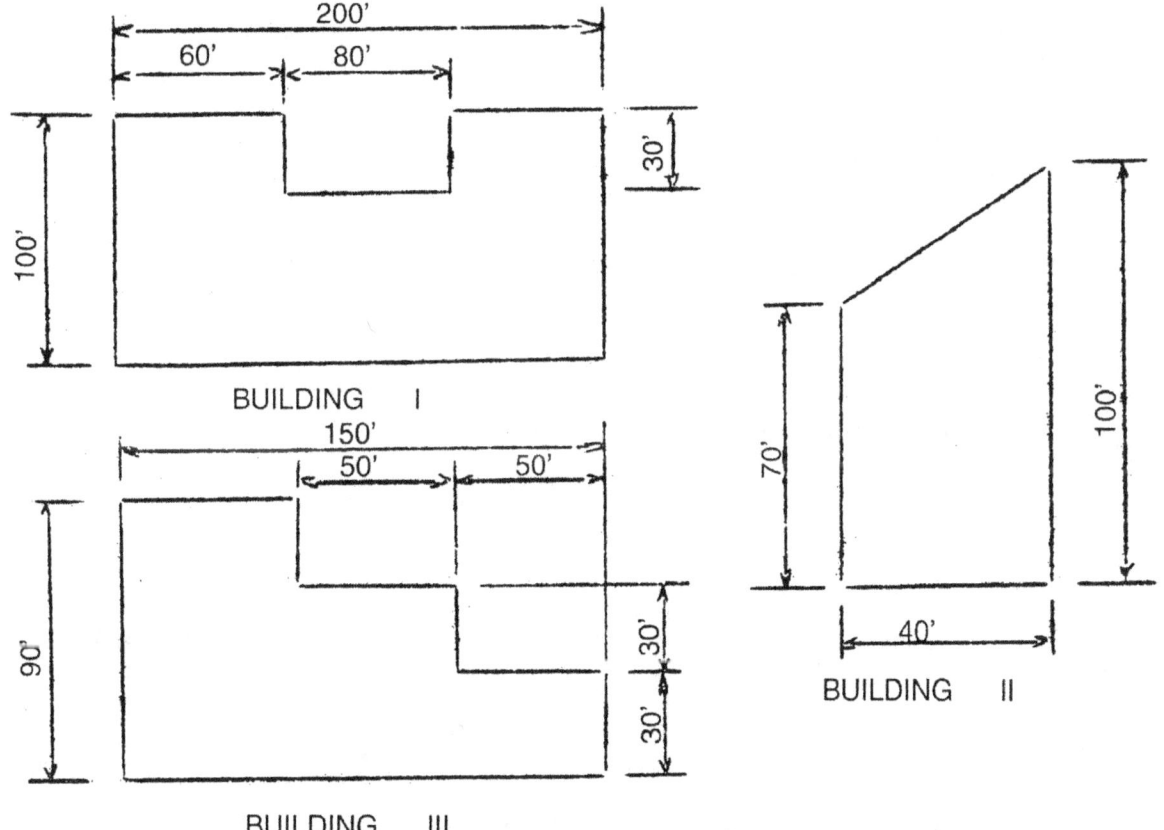

38. The *total* area on each floor of building I is, most nearly, _____ sq. ft.   38._____

    A. 17,000   B. 17,600   C. 20,000   D. 22,400

39. The *total* area on each floor of building II is, most nearly, _____ sq. ft.   39._____

    A. 3,400   B. 3,700   C. 4,000   D. 5,000

40. The *total* area on each floor of building III is, most nearly, _____ sq. ft.   40._____

   A. 9,000   B. ,0,500   C. 12,000   D. 13,500

41. The BEST method to use to determine the presence of hidden leaks in a metered water piping system in a dwelling is to   41._____

   A. test the pressure at first and second floor faucets and observe the difference in flow
   B. test the pressure at the house inlet and see whether there is a pressure drop from the main
   C. shut all outlets and see whether or not the meter registers
   D. compare each water bill with the average of that for the previous three periods

42. The PRINCIPAL reason for using a ballcock in a roof tank is to   42._____

   A. provide a positive shut-off of water
   B. prevent overflow of water
   C. eliminate clogging of valves
   D. reduce pressure losses

43. The MAIN reason for the use of a vacuum breaker in the supply line to a fixture is to   43._____

   A. eliminate back siphonage
   B. permit a freer flow of water
   C. prevent waste of water
   D. stop water hammer

44. Freezing of buried service lines on cold nights is BEST prevented by   44._____

   A. opening faucets and permitting the water to run
   B. applying heat to the pipes by means of a torch
   C. laying the pipes 4 feet below the surface
   D. insulating the lines with 85% magnesium

45. The rules state that the distance between a hub and a wet connection shall be a *minimum* of   45._____

   A. 6"   B. 12"   C. 18"   D. 24"

46. The tip of a faucet must be at least one inch above the flood rim level of the basin. This is required *principally* to prevent   46._____

   A. loss in water pressure   B. contamination
   C. leakage   D. breakage

47. When a wet connection is abandoned, the connection is   47._____

   A. left available for future use
   B. temporarily shut
   C. sealed with plumber's solder
   D. destroyed so that it can not be used again

48. The *maximum* number of buildings which a tap on a water main may serve is: 48._____

   A. 1   B. 2   C. 3   D. 4

49. The size and number of taps or connections for a supply service to a building is based on the

    A. total floor area of the building
    B. volume of the building
    C. height of the building
    D. number of floors in the building

50. A connection for commercial purposes may be made from a metered sprinkler line *provided* the connection is

    A. independently metered
    B. as large as the sprinkler line
    C. made in at least two places to the sprinkler line
    D. at least 3/4 the size of the sprinkler line

51. A valve that *must* be installed where there is a direct water connection to a refrigerator, and the unit has a capacity of more than 20 pounds of refrigerant, is a(n)

    A. swing   B. relief   C. angle   D. needle

52. In a direct water connection to the condenser of a refrigeration system, the water system has contact with the refrigerant. The valve which must be installed in this water piping system ahead of the condenser is a

    A. globe   B. gate   C. check   D. butterfly

53. Relative to the use of second-hand pipe for the repair of a service line, the rules state that

    A. the pipe must be thoroughly cleaned and sterilzed first
    B. the pipe must be inspected by the department of water supply, gas and electricity before it may be re-used
    C. only wrought iron pipe may be re-used for a service line
    D. second-hand pipe may not be re-used for a service line

54. Lead pipe may *not* be used for service lines when the diameter is greater than

    A. 1"   B. 2"   C. 3"   D. 4"

55. Brass pipe may *not* be used for service lines when the water is supplied from

    A. the Catskill system   B. the Croton system
    C. the Delaware system   D. a system of wells

56. A permissible mixture to be used when making up lead-lined fittings is

    A. litharge and glycerine   B. red lead and drier
    C. zinc filings and muriatic acid   D. borax and water

57. The house control valve must be a(n) _____ valve.

    A. gate   B. globe   C. check   D. angle

58. A curb valve is required on all fire service pipes and on all other pipes the diameter of which is *greater than*

    A. 1"   B. 2"   C. 3"   D. 4"

59. A gooseneck or swing offset at the connection of a service pipe to a tap is *not* required when the service pipe is made of

    A. brass
    B. galvanized iron
    C. cast iron
    D. cement-lined standard iron

60. The minimum size of a service pipe, as compared to the size of the tap controlling it, *shall be*

    A. one size smaller
    B. the same size
    C. one size larger
    D. two sizes larger

61. For a one- or two-family house, the *minimum* size of service pipe permitted is

    A. 5/8"
    B. 3/4"
    C. 1"
    D. 1 1/4"

62. A surge tank *would be* used in connection with a

    A. roof tank
    B. low pressure main
    C. flow meter
    D. large pump

Questions 63-67.

DIRECTIONS: Questions 63 to 67 are to be answered according to the diagram below.

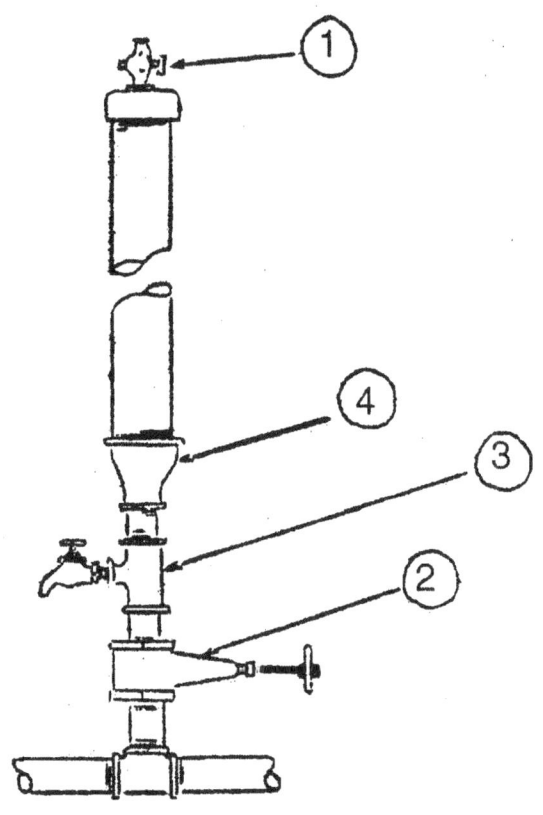

63. The item shown in the diagram above is a(n)

    A. flushometer
    B. air chamber
    C. venturi meter
    D. dash pot

64. The type of valve indicated by the number 1 in the diagram above is a(n)

    A. pet   B. angle   C. swing   D. butterfly

65. The type of valve indicated top the number 2 in the diagram above is a(n)

    A. check   B. relief   C. expansion   D. gate

66. The item indicated by the number 3 in the diagram above is a

    A. union   B. reducer   C. tee   D. coupling

67. The item indicated by the number 4 in the diagram above is a

    A. reducer   B. bell   C. bowl   D. flange

68. The PRINCIPAL *disadvantage of* a current type meter is that

    A. low velocity flow may not be recorded
    B. it cannot handle high velocity flow
    C. it is difficult to calibrate it
    D. it is more expensive than other types

69. The rules state that, when using a certain type of meter, there must be a straight section of pipe 8 times the diameter of the meter between the control valve and the meter. The type of meter referred to is a(n)

    A. disc
    B. oscillating piston
    C. current
    D. duplex

70. The city water supply myst be metered when it supplies an air conditioning system with a capacity *in excess of* _____ ton.

    A. 1/4   B. 1/3   C. 1/2   D. 3/4

71. Fire service meters are built similar to _____ meters.

    A. disc
    B. oscillating piston
    C. current
    D. compound

72. A corporation cock would be used along with a

    A. turbine meter
    B. wet connection
    C. crossover
    D. developed length

73. The one of the following pumps that *usually* requires priming is a

    A. piston   B. gear   C. rotary   D. centrifugal

74. The older style disc meters cannot be used for metering hot water because

    A. vapor lock will stop the meter
    B. the volume of hot water is different than that of cold water
    C. the disc is damaged by hot water
    D. hot water will fog the dial face

75. The purpose of a gooseneck is to

    A. provide support for the pipe
    B. permit expansion and contraction
    C. relieve sudden pressure
    D. make the connection easier

Questions 76-80.

DIRECTIONS: Questions 76 to 80, inclusive, refer to the following diagram:

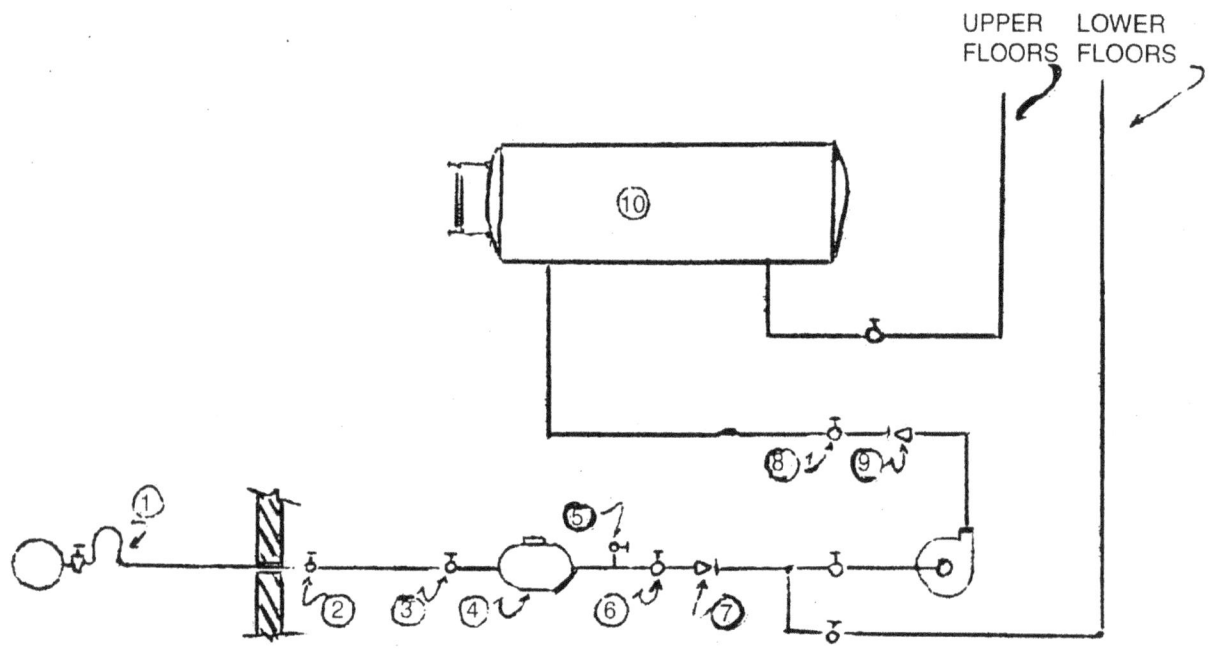

76. The water supply system illustrated in the diagram that appears on the preceding page is a _____ system.

    A. gravity
    B. hot and cold water
    C. down feed
    D. combined hydropneumatic-gravity

77. The purpose of the tank indicated by number 10 in the diagram on the preceding page is to

    A. maintain uniform pressure
    B. heat the water
    C. dose the water with chemicals
    D. prevent water hammer

78. The purpose of the fitting indicated by number 5 in the diagram on the preceding page is to

    A. bleed the line
    B. check the meter by flow test
    C. provide a connection for future needs
    D. relieve excess pressure

79. The fitting that is *not* necessary when the system draws water from only one main is indicated by the number

79.____

    A. 3 B. 6 C. 7 D. 9

80. When facing the water main, the gooseneck indicated must be laid

80.____

    A. to the left
    B. in a vertical plane with the gooseneck up
    C. in a vertical plane with the gooseneck down
    D. to the right

KEY (CORRECT ANSWERS)

1.	D	21.	C	41.	C	61.	B
2.	C	22.	D	42.	B	62.	D
3.	C	23.	C	43.	A	63.	B
4.	C	24.	B	44.	C	64.	A
5.	A	25.	C	45.	D	65.	D
6.	B	26.	A	46.	B	66.	C
7.	B	27.	B	47.	D	67.	A
8.	C	28.	C	48.	A	68.	A
9.	D	29.	D	49.	A	69.	C
10.	C	30.	C	50.	A	70.	B
11.	B	31.	D	51.	B	71.	D
12.	C	32.	D	52.	C	72.	B
13.	D	33.	D	53.	D	73.	D
14.	D	34.	B	54.	B	74.	C
15.	B	35.	C	55.	D	75.	B
16.	C	36.	B	56.	A	76.	D
17.	A	37.	B	57.	A	77.	A
18.	C	38.	B	58.	B	78.	B
19.	C	39.	A	59.	C	79.	C
20.	D	40.	A	60.	C	80.	D

EXAMINATION SECTION
TEST 1

DIRECTIONS: Each question or incomplete statement is followed by several suggested answers or completions. Select the one that BEST answers the question or completes the statement. *PRINT THE LETTER OF THE CORRECT ANSWER IN THE SPACE AT THE RIGHT.*

1. The diameter of the tap *usually* determines the

    A. pressure in the main
    B. diameter of the service pipe
    C. size of the main
    D. size of the water meter

    1.____

2. Generally, the use of water is LEAST between the hours of

    A. 9 a.m. and 12 noon
    B. 1 a.m. to 4 a.m.
    C. 4 p.m. to 7 p.m.
    D. 6 a.m. to 9 a.m.

    2.____

3. The disease that is *most likely* to be spread by means of a polluted water supply is

    A. malaria   B. cancer
    C. typhoid fever   D. common cold

    3.____

4. Water demand load for commercial and industrial use is *usually* determined on the basis of the

    A. size of the water service pipe
    B. water pressure
    C. building floor area
    D. number of floors in the building

    4.____

5. Water consumption is measured by a water

    A. service pipe   B. meter
    C. conduit   D. tank

    5.____

6. The one of the following chemicals which is used to soften water is

    A. calcium sulphate   B. magnesium carbonate
    C. sodium chloride   D. slaked lime

    6.____

7. Unless there is an emergency or the department of water supply, gas and electricity gives permission, no hydrant shall be used when the temperature is less than 32 degrees Fahrenheit.
    The basis for this ruling is:

    A. This temperature is below the freezing point of water, resulting in freezing of hose connections
    B. Water freezes at this temperature

    7.____

73

C. The valve steam may crack at this temperature
D. The drip valve of the hydrant will not operate at this temperature, resulting in flooding of the hydrant

8. Using a hpse to water a lawn is usually forbidden from November 1 to March 31. The *most important* reason for this prohibition is to

   A. reduce unnecessary use of water
   B. avoid hazards due to ice formation on the lawn
   C. avoid freezing of the water in the hose
   D. avoid dangerous reduction in water main pressure

8.____

9. A building is equipped with a one-inch water meter. The size refers to the

   A. inside diameter of the meter inlet pipe
   B. diameter of the meter disc
   C. loss of head in inches
   D. maximum flow in cubic inches per second

9.____

10. A bibb seat reamer is *most probably* required when

    A. a faucet is leaking
    B. a hose cannot be screwed tightly to a hose bib
    C. there is a burr on the inside of the cur pipe
    D. a tap has become plugged

10.____

11. If there is a constant leak from a flush tank into the bowl of a water closet, it is *probably* due to

    A. the ball cock jammed shut
    B. lift wire disconnected from the handle lever
    C. a hole in the copper float
    D. a defective shut-off valve

11.____

12. When a building is to be altered or erected, the water used in construction is

    A. metered if the building is more than six stories high
    B. metered if the building is less than six stories high
    C. not metered unless the building is eight or more stories high
    D. not metered if the building is to be used for dwelling purposes

12.____

13. With reference to water supply, the term "peak load" *usually* refers to:

    A. Height of structures to be supplied with water
    B. Elevation of water supply
    C. Hate of maximum demand
    D. Capacity of pressure regulating valves

13.____

14. A cubic foot of water is equal to about _____ gallons.

    A. 5 1/4   B. 7 1/2   C. 6   D. 8 1/2

14.____

15. One pound per square inch pressure of water will raise water to a height of

   A. 2.3 feet
   B. 18 inches
   C. 14.7 feet
   D. 4.5 feet

16. When the hub end of a soil pipe is to be sealed off, the *proper* fitting to use is a

   A. lug
   B. saddle
   C. cap
   D. plug

17. In water piping work, the term "riser" refers to

   A. a horizontal supply line
   B. hot water lines only
   C. cold water lines only
   D. a vertical supply line

18. The purpose of a check valve is to

   A. check excessive pressure of water
   B. allow water to flow one way only
   C. prevent sediment from backing into service pipe
   D. check trapped air in water pipe

19. The thread of a pipe with a male thread is

   A. on the inside of the pipe
   B. on the outside of the pipe
   C. inside and outside the pipe
   D. less likely to be damaged than the thread of a pipe with a female thread

20. Resistance to flow of water is *least* in a(n)

   A. angle valve
   B. pressure reducing valve
   C. globe valve
   D. gate valve

Questions 21 - 22.

Questions 21 and 22 are based on the following diagram.

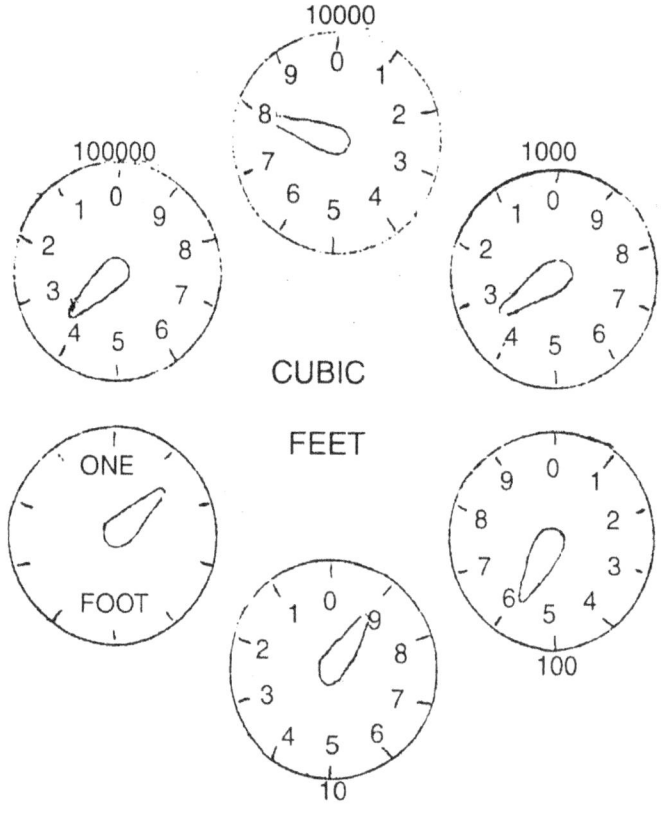

21. The water meter reading shown in the sketch, in cubic feet, is 21.____

    A. 373,591 B. 68,449 C. 37,359 D. 173,359

22. The pointer which does not appear in a correct position is on the dial labeled 22.____

    A. 1,000 B. 10,000 C. 10 D. 100

23. Assume that the current meter reading on the meter used in Question 21 is 8,947 cubic feet. The last reading was 81,732 cubic feet. 23.____
    It is obvious that

    A. consumption amounted to 72,785 feet
    B. the meter has been tampered with
    C. the meter is not recording properly
    D. consumption amounted to 27,215 cubic feet

24. Hot water meters should *not* be used on cold water lines because they 24.____

    A. will not measure cold water flows accurately
    B. will be injured by cold water flow
    C. cost far more than cold water meters
    D. are designed for intermittent water flows and not for a continuous supply

25. In an inspection of a water meter, it is found that the meter seals have been tampered with. The inspector should

   A. take the meter reading and then report the matter to his superior
   B. discuss the matter with the user and then warn him that the water supply may be shut off
   C. determine probable usage during the current period and then reset the meter to give an appropriate reading
   D. shut the inlet valve, place a seal upon it, and report the matter to his superior

26. An inspector finds that a water supply connection has been made to a house service pipe at a point between the basement wall and the water meter. This will result in

   A. contamination of the water supply
   B. excessive meter readings
   C. meter readings less than actual consumption
   D. waste of water

Questions 27 - 31.

Questions 27 to 31 refer to the diagram below.

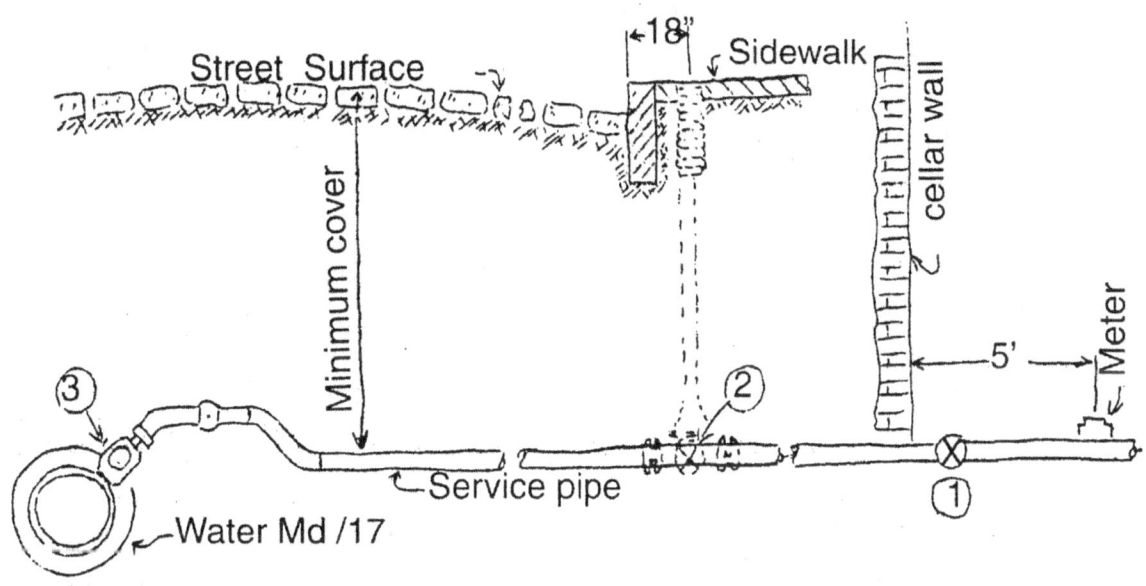

HOUSE SERVICE CONNECTION TO WATER MAIN

27. The device numbered (1) in the diagram is *probably* a _____ valve.

   A. check   B. foot
   C. gate   D. angle

28. The minimum cover for service pipe is specified as 4 feet. The *most important* reason for this requirement is to

   A. prevent freezing of water in service pipe
   B. avoid tampering with water supply or possible pollution of service line
   C. provide proper drainage in case of a leak
   D. provide a firm backfill to avoid breaking of connection between the water main and service pipe

29. Item numbered (2) in the diagram is a(n)

   A. corporation cock
   B. curb cock
   C. angle valve
   D. pressure reducing valve

30. Item numbered (3) in the diagram is a

   A. reducer
   B. reducing flange
   C. corporation cock
   D. service tee

31. Assume that a leak in the house service has been located in the pipe line beneath the sidewalk near the building line. To stop any further water loss until repairs are made, the *proper* procedure to follow is to close

   A. the valve at (1)
   B. the valve at (2)
   C. valves on the water main from which the service pipe leads
   D. all water outlets in the building

32. Each new service pipe shall be laid in a straight line at right angles to the street main. The BEST reason for this requirement is that it

   A. minimizes leakage at joints
   B. simplifies location of the service pipe under the sidewalk
   C. requires the shortest length of pipe
   D. permits the greatest flow of water

33. Water is flowing into a cylindrical tank at the rate of four cubic feet per minute. The time it will take to fill the tank whose dimensions are seven feet in height and four feet in diameter is *about*

   A. 22 minutes
   B. one-half hour
   C. 15 minutes
   D. one hour

34. The term "head" as used in relation to the flow of water can also be expressed as

   A. rate of flow
   B. resistance of pipe to water flow
   C. gallons per second
   D. water pressure

35. The flow of water in a pipe in cubic feet per second is equal to the

   A. diameter of the pipe in feet multiplied by the velocity in feet per second
   B. area of the pipe in square feet divided by the rate of flow in feet per second
   C. diameter of the pipe in feet divided by rate of flow in feet per second
   D. area of the pipe in square feet multiplied by the velocity in feet per second

36. To check a water meter to see whether it is registering, the procedure to follow is to

   A. turn the water off
   B. check the movement of the pointer of the dial of highest capacity
   C. check the movement of the pointer of the dial of lowest capacity
   D. remove the face of the meter to see if the gears are in motion

Questions 37 - 38.

Questions 37 and 38 are based upon the diagram below.

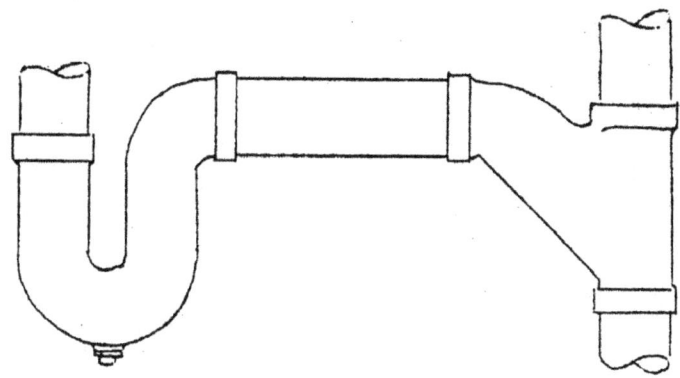

37. The trap shown in the diagram is *commonly* called a

    A. P-trap B. s-trap
    C. mechanical trap D. Y-trap

37.____

38. The function of this trap is to

    A. prevent inflow of air into soil pipe
    B. prevent backflow of sewer gas
    C. collect all wastes in the bottom of the trap
    D. prevent water from backing up into the water fixture

38.____

39. The purpose of a float and float switch in a roof tank is to

    A. keep the tank full
    B. close off the roof supply when water pressure is low
    C. vary pressure with the demand of the lower floors
    D. provide water for fire protection

39.____

40. The average pressure of water in the water mains in the city is *about* _____ lbs. per square inch.

    A. 50   B. 25   C. 95   D. 18

40.____

Questions 41 - 45.

The fittings represented in Column I on the following page are commonly found in water supply lines in a building. Select the correct name from Column II for the fitting in Column I and place the letter representing your choice next to the number of the fitting on your answer sheet.

Column I	Column II
41. [image of cap]	A. bushing
	B. union
	C. coupling
42. [image of coupling]	D. cap
	E. plug
43. [image of nipple]	F. nipple
	G. reducer
44. [image of bushing]	
45. [image of union]	

41. ____
42. ____
43. ____
44. ____
45. ____

46. Where a meter is used to measure water consumption, the charge for water is   46.____

    A. fifteen cents per hundred cubic feet
    B. fifteen cents per thousand cubic feet
    C. $1.50 per hundred cubic feet
    D. seventy-five cents per hundred cubic feet

47. The discs of positive displacement-type water meters are *usually* made of   47.____

    A. hardwood   B. metal alloys
    C. hard rubber   D. bronze

48. After you have read a meter, the owner tells you that he will be unable to pay the bill on time and asks you what will happen.   48.____
You *should* tell him that

    A. you just read the meter; after that, it is up to the office
    B. you will report the matter to your superior
    C. if he fails to pay before the end of next month he will be charged interest on the bill
    D. the city's financial position is not good and he should make every effort to pay the bill

49. You find that the meter glass is so dirty that the meter cannot be read. Department regulations provide that 49.____

    A. the supply shall be shut off until the meter is placed in good order
    B. the glass will be cleaned and leaky spindles packed without charge
    C. the meter be removed and replaced temporarily by a straight piece of pipe
    D. the owner be fined because the meter was allowed to become unsuitable

Questions 50 - 51.

Questions 50 and 51 are based on the table of frontage rates listed below.
The annual frontage rents on premises wholly or partly unmetered shall be as follows:

Front Width of Building:	One-Story
16 feet and under	$ 6.00
Over 16 feet, up to and including 18 feet	7.50
Over 18 feet, up to and including 20	9.00
Over 20 feet, up to and including 22 1/2 feet	10.50
Over 22 1/2 feet, up to and including 25 feet	12.00
Over 25 feet, up to and including 30 feet	15.00
Over 30 feet, up to and including 37 1/2 feet	18.00
Over 37 1/2 feet, up to and including 50 feet	21.00

For each additional story $1.50 per annum shall be added; and for each additional ten (10) feet or part thereof above fifty (50) feet in front width of building, #3 shall be added.

The apportionment of the regular frontage rates upon buildings shall be on the basis that but one family is to occupy same, and for each additional family or apartment, $1.50 per year shall be charged.

Baths in excess of one (1) to each house, $4.50 per annum.

Shower bath, not installed over bath tubs, and "sitz" baths shall be charged same as baths.

50. Based on the above data, the annual water charge for a 2-story, 1-family dwelling, 20 feet wide, is 50.____

    A. $9.00   B. $10.50   C. $13.50   D. $15.00

51. Based on the above data, the annual water charge for a 2-story, 1-family dwelling, 24 feet wide, is 51.____

    A. $12.00   B. $13.50   C. $16.30   D. $18.00

52. Gaskets are *usually* used to 52.____

    A. make caulked joints leak-proof
    B. seal threaded joints
    C. make flanged joints pressure tight
    D. reduce possible breaking of joints due to water hammer pressure

53. The fitting used to close off the threaded male end of a line is a

   A. bushing
   B. union
   C. plug
   D. cap

54. To take a right-angle line from a horizontal or vertical run of pipe, the fitting to use is a

   A. tee
   B. 90° elbow
   C. 60 Y-bend
   D. cross

55. An inspector is told by the owner of a factory that his water bill is excessive and that his use of water was about the same as the previous year when the bill was lower. The inspector *should*

   A. make an immediate floor-to-floor survey to detect sources of water waste
   B. suggest a waste survey by the owner or his plumber
   C. suggest that the owner's statement is probably not correct, as evidenced by the meter reading
   D. suggest that a new meter by installed

56. An additional toilet has been installed in the basement of a small private residence. It is *correct* to say that water charges will

   A. *not* be changed unless there is an increased use of water
   B. be increased because an additional fixture has been installed
   C. be changed only if such installation is the result of an increase in the number of inhabitants of the dwelling
   D. *not* be changed because such buildings usually have a metered supply

Questions 57 - 59.

Questions 57 to 59 inclusive refer to the paragraph below.

Part of a section of the Administrative Code relating to the placing of water meters ptates:

"This section shall not be CONSTRUED so as to REMIT or prevent the due collection of arrearages or charges for water consumption heretofore INCURRED, nor interfere with the proper liens therefor, nor of charges, or rates, or liens hereafter incurred for water consumption in any building or place which may not contain one of the meters aforesaid."

57. The word "construed" underlined in this paragraph means, *most nearly*,

   A. delayed
   B. mistaken
   C. enacted
   D. interpreted

58. The word "remit" as used in this paragraph means, *most nearly*,

   A. send out
   B. dispense with
   C. settle
   D. justify

59. The word "incurred" underlined in this paragraph means, *most nearly*,

   A. credited with
   B. discharged
   C. accounted for
   D. liable for

60. While making a meter reading, an inspector notices some defects in the water supply line. He suggests corrections to the property owner. The grateful owner insists that the inspector accept a gratuity.
The inspector *should*

   A. accept the gratuity with the understanding that the money will be forwarded to the city treasurer
   B. accept the gratuity since he has assisted the owner beyond his regular duty
   C. refuse the gratuity because acceptance is a violation of department regulations
   D. refuse the gratuity because acceptance would mean that he has not taken a proper reading

61. An inspector, sent to obtain meter readings, is refused admission to the premises.
His *next* step should be to

   A. recommend that the water supply to the premises be shut off
   B. report the refusal to his superior for further action
   C. obtain the assistance of the police to force access to the meter
   D. recommend using the average consumption for the last three periods to determine the current charge

62. A tenant informs an inspector of water consumption that there is a definite hazard due to leakage of illuminating gas in the hallway and cellar of the building. The *most appropriate* procedure to follow is to

   A. advise the tenant that the owner will be informed of the possible hazard
   B. tell the tenant that he has no jurisdiction
   C. make a soap test to locate the gas leak
   D. notify the Police Department, advising them of the situation

63. An inspection of a tenant's complaint reveals several neglected leaks in water supply fixtures and lines. The, owner of the small tenement building tells you that he'll take care of the matter in due time and that, since he is paying for the water used in the form of water taxes, it is not really your concern. Your answer *should be* that

   A. the water tax will be increased if the waste caused by the leaks is not corrected
   B. the water supply may be contaminated through leakage
   C. his statement is correct, but that the water is being wasted nevertheless
   D. his statement is not correct, since his water supply is not metered

64. An inspector notices a sawed-off shotgun in the basement of an office building. This is an illegal weapon and no permits are issued by the Police Department for its use.
The inspector *should*

   A. notify the building superintendent of his discovery
   B. ignore the gun, since he has no jurisdiction at all
   C. notify the local precinct station of the Police Department
   D. send a report about the gun to the main office of the department of water supply, gas and electricity

65. An inspector, who has just completed an inspection, is stopped on the street by a man who asks him for information about the economic status of the owner and the condition of the property.
    The inspector's action *should be* to

    A. cooperate with this man and give him the desired information to the best of his knowledge
    B. refer the man to the main office for the desired information
    C. suggest that the man discuss the matter with the owner himself
    D. tell him about the condition of the property and refer him to the nearest commercial bank for information as to the owner's economic status

66. The *most important* reason for avoiding the use of lead pipe for water supply lines in a building is that it

    A. tends to sag and become deformed
    B. cracks easily in cold weather
    C. interferes with flow due to formation of lead compounds
    D. is corroded readily by electrolysis

67. The new owner of a small residence writes to the department of water supply, gas and electricity asking for a refund since he was away from home during the summer months. His request was denied.
    The *basis* for the denial of refund is:

    A. The water charge is fixed as of conditions on January 1, and is valid for the entire year whether the water is used or not
    B. The water charge may not be refunded in part unless the owner filed a formal notice and had the service connection sealed off
    C. There is no way of determining how much water was actually used during the year
    D. Water waste might have occurred during the period the dwelling was closed

68. A person who intends to close his house for three months during the summer should

    A. notify the department
    B. make a waste survey before so doing
    C. shut off the main house control valve
    D. do nothing if all fixtures are in good repair

69. In your inspection of a house you notice that a faucet is leaking.
    Of the following, the *most probable* cause for the leak is:

    A. uneven seat
    B. corrosion of the supply pipe
    C. excessive water pressure
    D. too little water pressure

70. The opening of a faucet extends below the overflow of a wash basin. The *principal* objection to this type of fixture is that

    A. the faucet end may become polluted
    B. water hammer is possible if the faucet is open when the basin is full
    C. back-siphonage is possible when the faucet is open and the basin is full
    D. a careless user is more likely to waste water

71. A meter may not be installed if it is more than one standard size larger than the tap or connection to the water main.
    The *reason* for this requirement is that

    A. if the meter is more than one standard size larger than the connection, it may not register small flows accurately
    B. the connection of a larger meter will result in higher friction losses
    C. the flow of water in the service pipe will be greatly increased
    D. too great a difference between the size of the supply line and the meter inlet makes connection difficult

71.____

72. A faucet in the basement of a tenement is leaking. Before this faucet can be repaired, it is *necessary* to shut off

    A. the service line where it enters the building
    B. all valves between the street and the faucet
    C. valve on the riser above the faucet
    D. the valve below the faucet

72.____

73. While reading a meter in a factory you hear much banging in the supply line. The superintendent tells you that the banging has been going on ever since flushometers were installed in the rest rooms.
    Department regulations require that

    A. the piping layout be altered to eliminate the noise
    B. nothing need be done
    C. the flushometers be removed
    D. an air chamber be installed

73.____

74. On an inspection of a meter in a commercial building, you see a man in the basement working on an oil burner. You do not know his identity or whether he is authorized to work in the building.
    The *most reasonable* thing to do is to

    A. pay no attention to the man and take the meter reading
    B. ignore him, but include a brief statement about him in your report
    C. challenge the man and obtain his identity
    D. watch him carefully to determine if his behavior is proper

74.____

75. The department of water supply, gas and electricity operates a high pressure fire system in some locations so that

    A. water may be available for fire fighting in areas of low elevation
    B. the water used for fire fighting will not freeze under high pressure
    C. manufacturing, business and waterfront sections may have extra protection
    D. water may be available for fire fighting in sections of high elevation

75.____

KEY (CORRECT ANSWERS)

1. D	16. D	31. B	46. A	61. B
2. B	17. D	32. B	47. C	62. D
3. C	18. B	33. A	48. C	63. C
4. A	19. B	34. D	49. B	64. C
5. B	20. D	35. D	50. B	65. C
6. D	21. C	36. C	51. D	66. A
7. B	22. B	37. A	52. C	67. A
8. A	23. D	38. B	53. D	68. C
9. A	24. A	39. A	54. A	69. A
10. A	25. A	40. A	55. B	70. C
11. C	26. C	41. D	56. B	71. A
12. A	27. B	42. C	57. D	72. D
13. C	28. A	43. F	58. B	73. D
14. B	29. B	44. A	59. D	74. A
15. A	30. C	45. B	60. C	75. C

MECHANICAL APTITUDE
MECHANICAL COMPREHENSION
EXAMINATION SECTION
TEST 1

DIRECTIONS: Each question or incomplete statement below is followed by several suggested answers or completions. Select the *one* that *BEST* answers the question or completes the statement. *PRINT THE LETTER OF THE CORRECT ANSWER IN THE SPACE AT THE RIGHT.*

Questions 1-3.

DIRECTIONS: Questions 1 to 3 inclusive are based upon the following paragraph.

The only openings permitted in fire partitions except openings for ventilating ducts shall be those required for doors. There shall be but one such door opening unless the provision of additional openings would not exceed, in total width of all doorways, 25 percent of the length of the wall. The minimum distance between openings shall be three feet. The maximum area for such a door opening shall be 80 square feet, except that such openings for the passage of motor trucks may be a maximum of 140 square feet.

1. According to the above paragraph, openings in fire partitions are permitted *only* for

   A. doors
   B. doors and windows
   C. doors and ventilation ducts
   D. doors, windows and ventilation ducts

2. In a fire partition, 22 feet long and 10 feet high, the *MAXIMUM* number of doors, 3 feet wide and 7 feet high, is

   A. 1 B. 2 C. 3 D. 4

3.
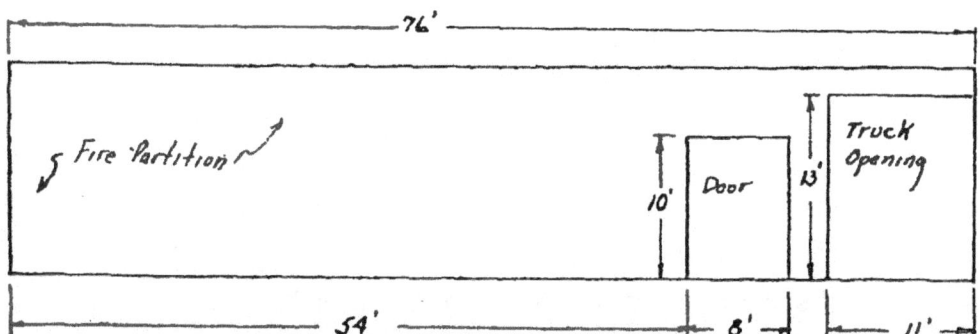

The *one* of the following statements about the layout shown above that is *MOST* accurate is that the

   A. total width of the openings is too large
   B. truck opening is too large
   C. truck and door openings are too close together
   D. layout is acceptable

4. At a given temperature, a wet hand will freeze to a bar of metal, but NOT to a piece of wood, because the

   A. metal expands and contracts more than the wood
   B. wood is softer than the metal
   C. wood will burn at a lower temperature than the metal
   D. metal is a better conductor of heat than the wood

5. Of the following items commonly found in a household, the one that uses the MOST electric current is a(n)

   A. 150-watt light bulb
   B. toaster
   C. door buzzer
   D. 8" electric fan

6. Sand and ashes are frequently placed on icy pavements to prevent skidding. The effect of the sand and ashes is to increase

   A. inertia   B. gravity   C. momentum   D. friction

7. The air near the ceiling of a room usually is warmer than the air near the floor because

   A. there is better air circulation at the floor level
   B. warm air is lighter than cold air
   C. windows usually are nearer the floor than the ceiling
   D. heating pipes usually run along the ceiling

8.

DIA. 1   DIA. 2

It is safer to use the ladder positioned as shown in diagram 1 than as shown in diagram 2 because, in diagram 1,

   A. less strain is placed upon the center rungs of the ladder
   B. it is easier to grip and stand on the ladder
   C. the ladder reaches a lower height
   D. the ladder is less likely to tip over backwards

9.

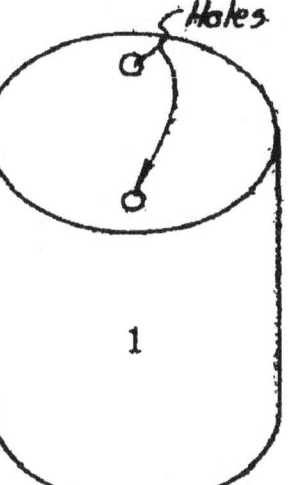 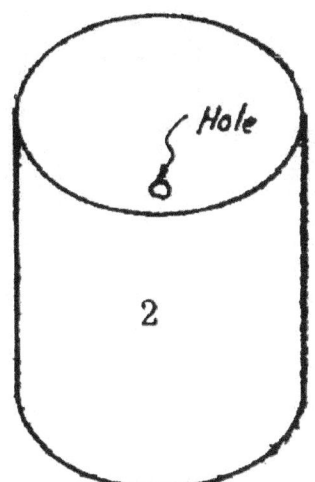

It is *easier* to pour a liquid from:

A. Can 1 because there are two holes from which the liquid can flow
B. Can 1 because air can enter through one hole while the liquid comes out the other hole
C. Can 2 because the liquid comes out under greater pressure
D. Can 2 because it is easier to direct the flow of the liquid when there is only one hole

10. A substance which is subject to "spontaneous combustion" is one that

A. is explosive when heated
B. is capable of catching fire without an external source of heat
C. acts to speed up the burning of material
D. liberates oxygen when heated

11. The sudden shutting down of a nozzle on a hose discharging water under high pressure is a *bad* practice CHIEFLY because the

A. hose is likely to whip about violently
B. hose is likely to burst
C. valve handle is likely to snap
D. valve handle is likely to jam

12. Fire can continue where there are present fuel, oxygen from the air or other source, and a sufficiently high temperature to maintain combustion. The method of extinguishment of fire MOST commonly used is to

A. remove the fuel
B. exclude the oxygen from the burning material
C. reduce the temperature of the burning material
D. smother the flames of the burning material

13.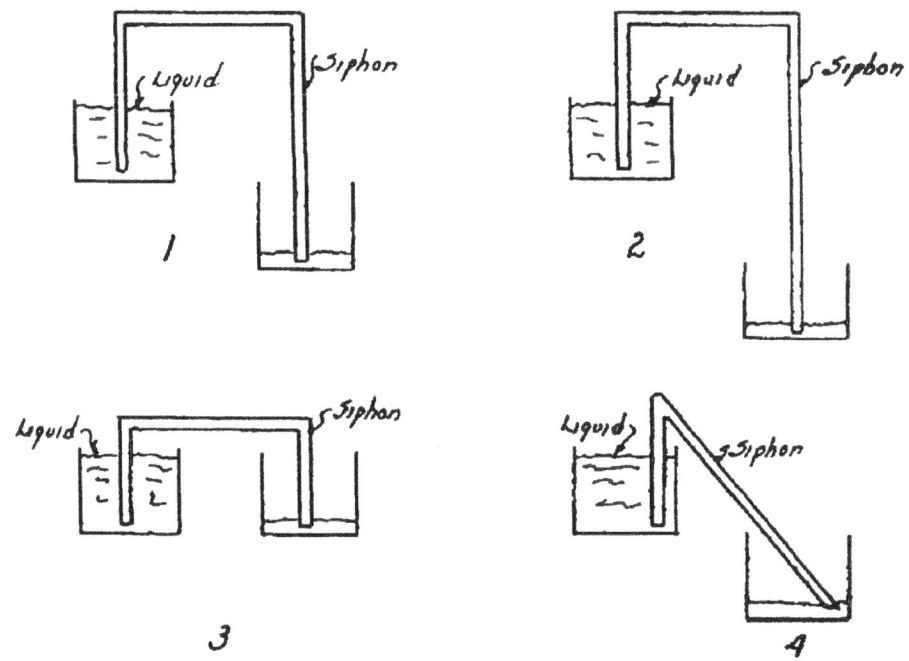

The one of the siphon arrangements shown above which would MOST quickly transfer a solution from the container on the left side to the one on the right side is numbered

A. 1   B. 2   C. 3   D. 4

14. Static electricity is a hazard in industry CHIEFLY because it may cause

A. dangerous or painful burns
B. chemical decomposition of toxic elements
C. sparks which can start an explosion
D. overheating of electrical equipment

15.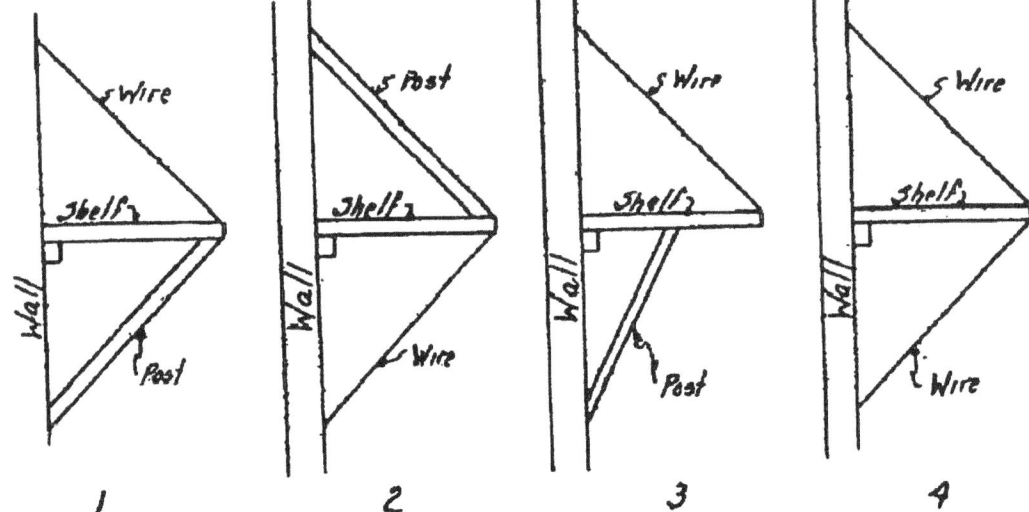

The STRONGEST method of supporting the shelf is shown in diagram

A. 1   B. 2   C. 3   D. 4

16. A row boat will float *deeper* in fresh water than in salt water *because* 16____

    A. in the salt water the salt will occupy part of the space
    B. fresh water is heavier than salt water
    C. salt water is heavier than fresh water
    D. salt water offers less resistance than fresh water

17. 17____

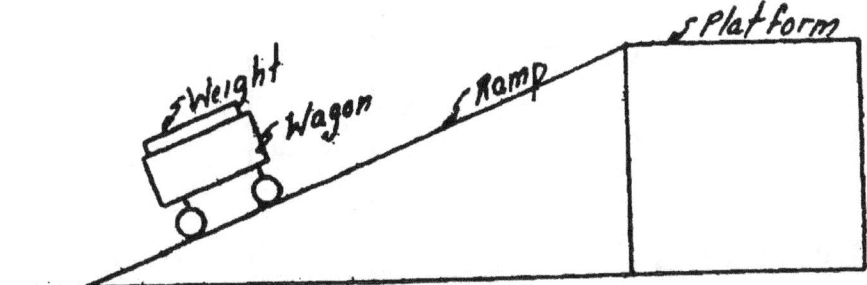

It is easier to get the load onto the platform by using the ramp than it is to lift it directly onto the platform. This is *true* because the effect of the ramp is to

    A. reduce the amount of friction so that less force is required
    B. distribute the weight over a larger area
    C. support part of the load so that less force is needed to move the wagon
    D. increase the effect of the moving weight

18. 18____

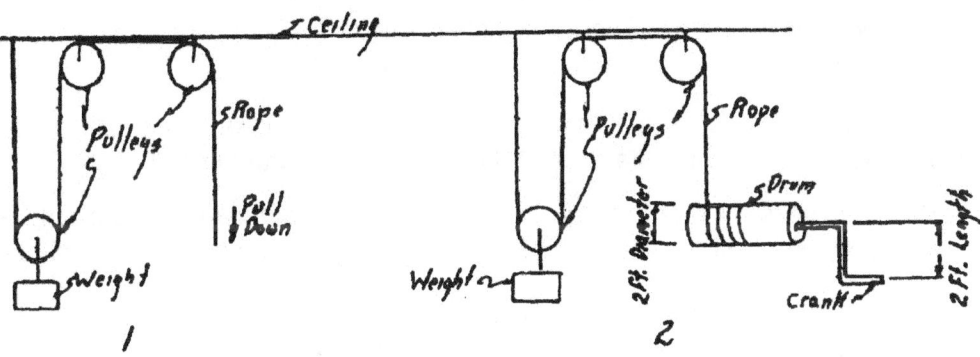

More weight can be lifted by the method shown in diagram 2 than as shown in diagram 1 because

    A. it takes less force to turn a crank than it does to pull in a straight line
    B. the drum will prevent the weight from falling by itself
    C. the length of the crank is larger than the radius of the drum
    D. the drum has more rope on it easing the pull

19.

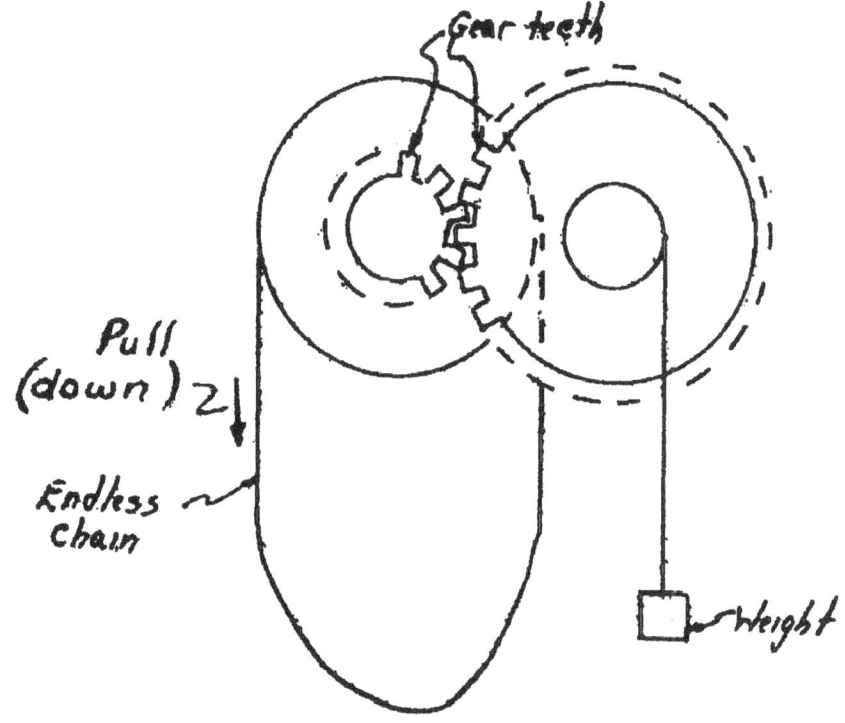

As the endless chain is pulled down in the direction shown, the weight will move

- A. *up* faster than the endless chain is pulled down
- B. *up* slower than the endless chain is pulled down
- C. *down* faster than the endless chain is pulled down
- D. *down* slower than the endless chain is pulled down

20. Two balls of the same size, but different weights, are both dropped from a 10-ft. height. The one of the following statements that is MOST accurate is that

- A. both balls will reach the ground at the same time because they are the same size
- B. both balls will reach the ground at the same time because the effect of gravity is the same on both balls
- C. the heavier ball will reach the ground first because it weighs more
- D. the lighter ball will reach the ground first because air resistance is greater on the heavier ball

21. It is considered poor practice to increase the leverage of a wrench by placing a pipe over the handle of the wrench. This is true PRINCIPALLY because

- A. the wrench may break
- B. the wrench may slip off the nut
- C. it is harder to place the wrench on the nut
- D. the wrench is more difficult to handle

22.

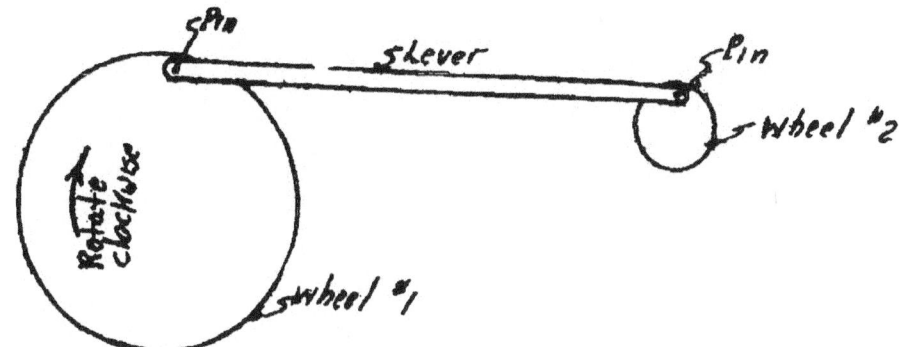

If wheel #1 is turned in the direction shown, wheel #2 will

A. turn continously in a clockwise direction
B. turn continously in a counterclockwise direction
C. move back and fourth
D. became jammed and both wheels will shop

23. ALL SOLID AREAS REPRESENT EQUAL WEIGHTS ATTACHED TO THE FLYWHEEL

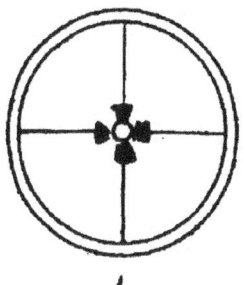 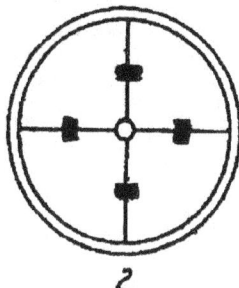 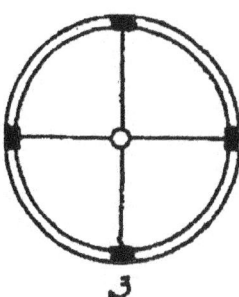

1   2   3

The above diagrams are of flywheels made of the same material with the same dimensions and attached to similar engines. The solid areas represent equal weights attached to the fly wheel. If all three engines are running at the same speed for the same length of time and the power to the engines is shut of simultaneously,

A. wheel 1 will continue turning longest
B. wheel 2 will continue turning longest
C. wheel 3 will continue turning longest
D. all three wheels will continue turning for the same time

24. The one of the following substance which expands when freezing is

A. alcohol   B. ammonia   C. mercury   D. water

25. A piece of copper wire 30 feet long is cut into two pieces, 20 feet and 10 feet. The resistance of the *longer* piece, compared to the shorter, is

A. one-half as much   B. two-thirds as much
C. one and one-half as much   D. twice as much

8 (#1)

KEY (CORRECT ANSWERS)

1. C
2. A
3. B
4. D
5. B

6. D
7. B
8. D
9. B
10. B

11. B
12. C
13. B
14. C
15. A

16. C
17. C
18. C
19. D
20. B

21. A
22. D
23. C
24. D
25. D

TEST 2

DIRECTIONS: Each question or incomplete statement below is followed by several suggested answers or completions. Select the *one* that *BEST* answers the question or completes the statement. *PRINT THE LETTER OF THE CORRECT ANSWER IN THE SPACE AT THE RIGHT.*

Questions 1-2.

DIRECTIONS: Questions 1 and 2 are to be answered in accordance with the information in the following statement:

The electrical resistance of copper wires varies directly with their lengths and inversely with their cross section areas.

1. A piece of copper wire 30 feet long is cut into two pieces, 20 feet and 10 feet. The resistance of the *longer* piece, compared to the shorter, is

    A. one-half as much
    B. two-thirds as much
    C. one and one-half as much
    D. twice as much

2. Two pieces of copper wire are each 10 feet long but the cross section area of one is 2/3 that of the other. The resistance of the piece with the *larger* cross-section area is

    A. one-half the resistance of the smaller
    B. two-thirds the resistance of the smaller
    C. one and one-half times the resistance of the smaller
    D. twice the resistance of the smaller

3.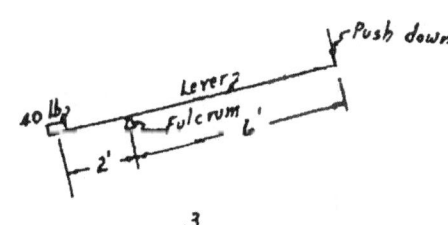

    The arrangement of the lever which would require the *LEAST* amount of force to move the weight is shown in the diagram numbered

    A. 1   B. 2   C. 3   D. 4

4. Steel supporting beams in buildings often are surrounded by a thin layer of concrete to keep the beams from becoming hot and collapsing during a fire.
The *one* of the following statements which *BEST* explains how collapse is prevented by this arrangement is that concrete

    A. becomes stronger as its temperature is increased

B. acts as an insulating material
C. protects the beam from rust and corrosion
D. reacts chemically with steel at high temperatures

5. If boiling water is poured into a drinking glass, the glass is likely to crack. If, however, a metal spoon first is placed in the glass, it is much less likely to crack. The reason that the glass with the spoon is *less likely* to crack is that the spoon

   A. distributes the water over a larger surface of the glass
   B. quickly absorbs heat from the water
   C. reinforces the glass
   D. reduces the amount of water which can be poured into the glass

6. It takes *more* energy to force water through a *long* pipe than through a *short* pipe of the same diameter. The PRINCIPAL reason for this is

   A. gravity   B. friction   C. inertia   D. cohesion

7. A pump, discharging at 300 lbs.-per-sq.-inch pressure, delivers water through 100 feet of pipe laid horizontally. If the valve at the end of the pipe is shut so that no water can flow, then the pressure at the valve is, for practical purposes,

   A. *greater* than the pressure at the pump
   B. *equal to* the pressure at the pump
   C. *less* than the pressure at the pump
   D. *greater or less* than the pressure at the pump, depending on the type of pump used

8. The explosive force of a gas when stored under various pressures is given in the following table:

Storage Pressure	Explosive Force
10	1
20	8
30	27
40	64
50	125

   The *one* of the following statements which BEST expresses the relationship between the storage pressure and explosive force is that
   A. there is no systematic relationship between an increase in storage pressure and an increase in explosive force
   B. the explosive force varies as the square of the pressure
   C. the explosive force varies as the cube of the pressure
   D. the explosive force varies as the fourth power of the pressure

9.

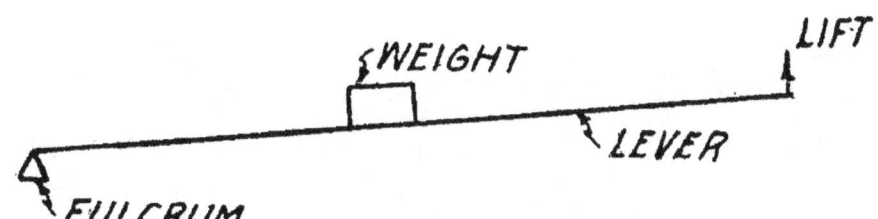

The leverage system in the sketch above is used to raise a weight. In order to *reduce* the amount of force required to raise the weight, it is necessary to

A. decrease the length of the lever
B. place the weight closer to the fulcrum
C. move the weight closer to the person applying the force
D. move the fulcrum further from the weight

10. In the accompanying sketch of a block and fall, if the end of the rope P is pulled so that it moves one foot, the distance the weight will be *raised* is
A. 1/2 ft.
B. 1 ft.
C. 1 1/2 ft.
D. 2 ft.

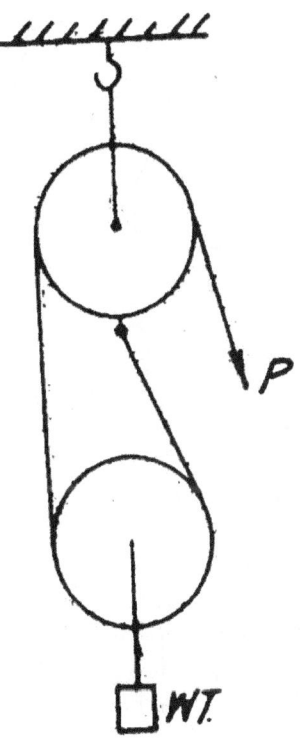

11.

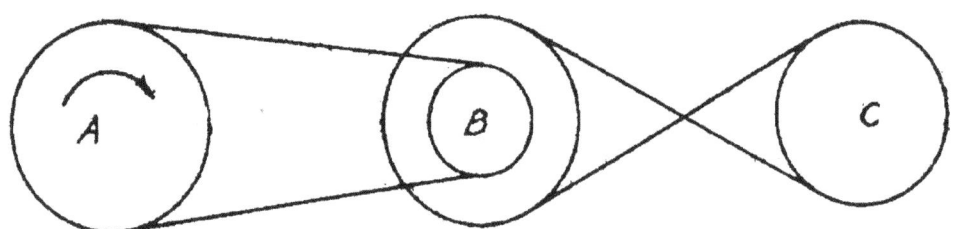

The above sketch diagrammatically shows a pulley and belt system. If pulley A is made to rotate in a clockwise direction, *then* pulley C will rotate

A. faster than pulley A and in a clockwise direction
B. slower than pulley A and in a clockwise direction
C. faster than pulley A and in a counter-clockwise direction
D. slower than pulley A and in a counter-clockwise direction

12.

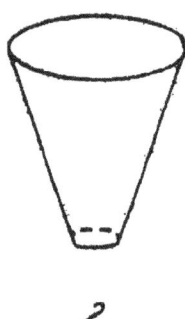 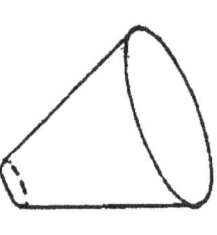 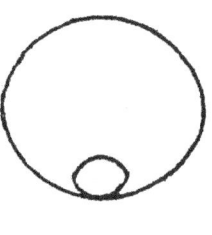

The above diagrams show four positions of the same object. The position in which this object is *MOST* stable is

A. 1 B. 2 C. 3 D. 4

13. The accompanying sketch diagrammatically shows a system of meshing gears with relative diameters as drawn. If gear 1 is made to rotate in the direction of the arrow, *then* the gear that will turn *FASTEST* is numbered

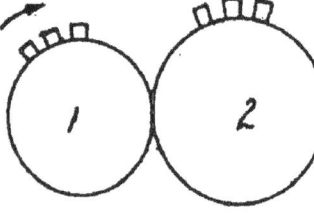 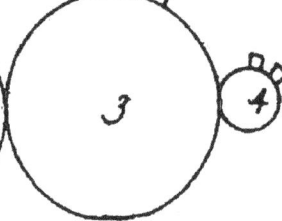

A. 1 B. 2 C. 3 D. 4

14.

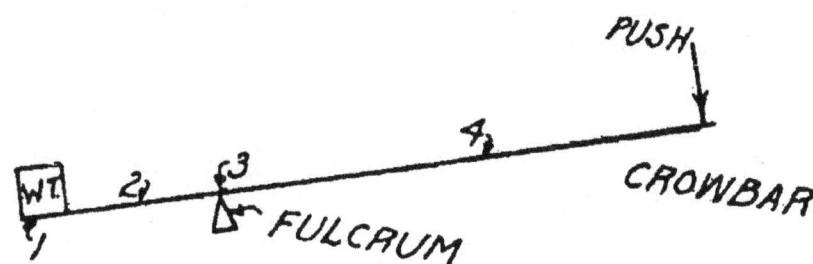

The above sketch shows a weight being lifted by means of a crowbar.
The point at which the tendency for the bar to break is GREATEST is

A. 1   B. 2   C. 3   D. 4

15.

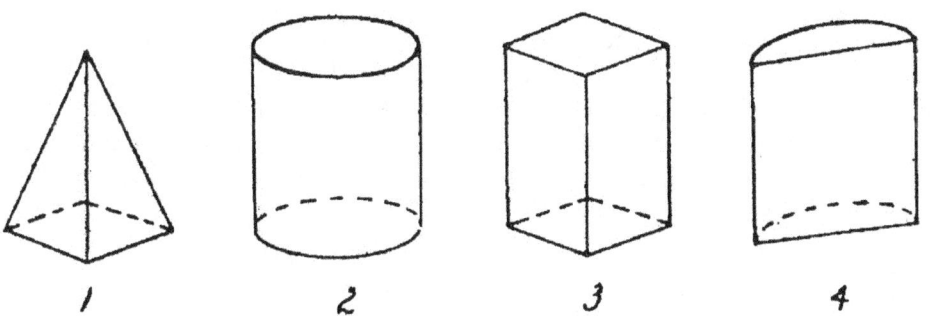

The above sketches show four objects which weigh the same but have different shapes.
The object which is MOST difficult to tip over is numbered

A. 1   B. 2   C. 3   D. 4

16.

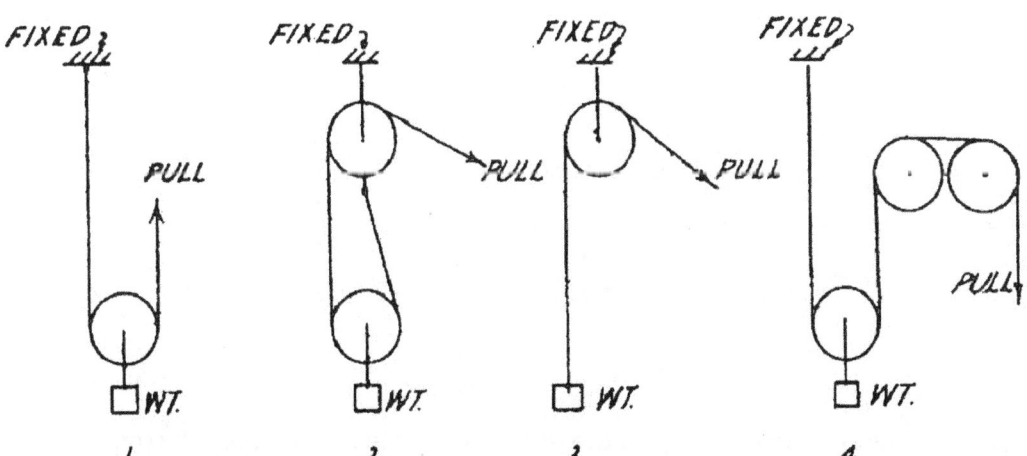

An object is to be lifted by means of a system of lines and pulleys. Of the systems shown above, the one which would require the GREATEST force to be used in lifting the weight is the one numbered

A. 1   B. 2   C. 3   D. 4

17. An intense fire develops in a room in which carbon dioxide cylinders are stored. The PRINCIPAL hazard in this situation is that

    A. the CO_2 may catch fire
    B. toxic fumes may be released
    C. the cylinders may explode
    D. released CO_2 may intensify the fire

18. At a fire involving the roof of a 5-story building, the firemen trained their hose stream on the fire from a vacant lot across the street, aiming the stream at a point about 15 feet above the roof.
    In this situation, water in the stream would be traveling at the GREATEST speed

    A. as it leaves the hose nozzle
    B. at a point midway between the ground and the roof
    C. at the maximum height of the stream
    D. as it drops on the roof

19. A principle of lighting is that the intensity of illumination at a point is inversely proportional to the square of the distance from the source of illumination.
    Assume that a pulley lamp is lowered from a position of 6 feet to one of three feet above a desk. According to the above principle, we would expect that the amount of illumination reaching the desk from the lamp in the lower position, as compared to the higher position, will be

    A. half as much   B. twice as much
    C. four times as much   D. nine times as much

20.

    1 *2* *3* *4*

    When standpipes are required in a structure, sufficient risers must be installed so that no point on the floor is more than 120 feet from a riser.
    The one of the above diagrams which gives the MAXIMUM area which can be covered by one riser is

    A. 1   B. 2   C. 3   D. 4

21. Spontaneous combustion may be the reason for a pile of oily rags catching fire.
    In general, spontaneous combustion is the DIRECT result of

    A. application of flame   B. falling sparks
    C. intense sunlight   D. chemical action
    E. radioactivity

22. In general, firemen are advised not to direct a solid stream of water on fires burning in electrical equipment. Of the following, the MOST logical reason for this instruction is that   22____
    A. water is a conductor of electricity
    B. water will do more damage to the electrical equipment than the fire
    C. hydrogen in water may explode when it comes in contact with electric current
    D. water will not effectively extinguish fires in electrical equipment
    E. water may spread the fire to other circuits

23. The height at which a fireboat will float in still water is determined CHIEFLY by the   23____
    A. weight of the water displaced by the boat
    B. horsepower of the boat's engines
    C. number of propellers on the boat
    D. curve the bow has above the water line
    E. skill with which the boat is maneuvered

24. When firemen are working at the nozzle of a hose they usually lean forward on the hose. The *most likely* reason for taking this position is that   24____
    A. the surrounding air is cooled, making the firemen more comfortable
    B. a backward force is developed which must be counteracted
    C. the firemen can better see where the stream strikes
    D. the fireman are better protected from injury by falling debris
    E. the stream is projected further

25. In general, the color and odor of smoke will BEST indicate   25____
    A. the cause of the fire
    B. the extent of the fire
    C. how long the fire has been burning
    D. the kind of material on fire
    E. the exact seat of the fire

KEY (CORRECT ANSWERS)

1. D
2. B
3. A
4. B
5. B

6. B
7. B
8. C
9. B
10. A

11. C
12. A
13. D
14. C
15. A

16. C
17. C
18. A
19. C
20. C

21. D
22. A
23. A
24. B
25. D

TEST 3

DIRECTIONS: Each question or incomplete statement below is followed by several suggested answers or completions. Select the *one* that *BEST* answers the question or completes the statement. *PRINT THE LETTER OF THE CORRECT ANSWER IN THE SPACE AT THE RIGHT.*

1. As a demonstration, firemen set up two hose lines identical in every respect except that one was longer than the other. Water was then delivered through these lines from one pump and it was seen that the stream from the longer hose line had a shorter "throw," Of the following, the *MOST* valid explanation of this difference in "throw" is that the

    A. air resistance to the water stream is proportional to the length of hose
    B. time required for water to travel through the longer hose is greater than for the shorter one
    C. loss due to friction is greater in the longer hose than in the shorter one
    D. rise of temperature is greater in the longer hose than in the shorter one
    E. longer hose line probably developed a leak at one of the coupling joints

2. Of the following toxic gases, the *one* which is *MOST* dangerous because it cannot be seen and has no odor, is

    A. ether   B. carbon monoxide   C. chlorine
    D. ammonia   E. cooking gas

3. You are visiting with some friends when their young son rushes into the room with his clothes on fire. You immediately wrap him in a rug and roll him on the floor. The *MOST* important reason for your action is that the

    A. flames are confined within the rug
    B. air supply to the fire is reduced
    C. burns sustained will be third degree, rather than first degree
    D. whirling action will put out the fire
    E. boy will not suffer from shock

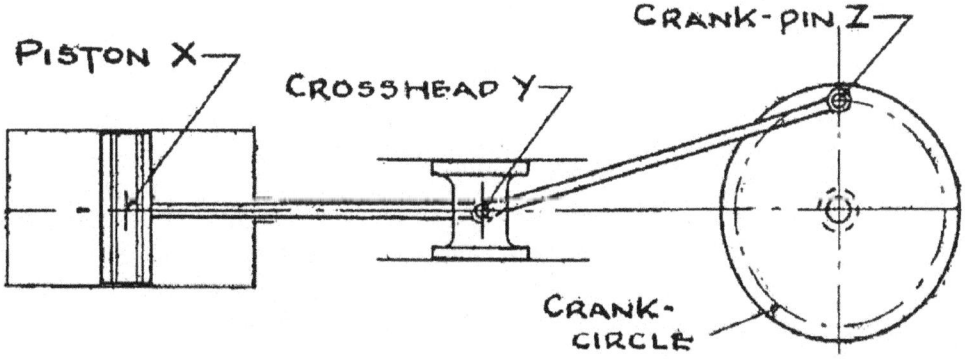

FIGURE I

2 (#3)

Questions 4-6,

DIRECTIONS: The device shown in Figure I above represents schematically a mechanism commonly used to change reciprocating (back and forth) motion to rotation (circular) motion.
The following questions, numbered 4 to 6 inclusive, are to be answered with reference to this device.

4. Assume that piston X is placed in its extreme left position so that X, Y and Z are in a horizontal line. If a horizontal force to the right is applied to the piston X, we may then expect that 4____

   A. the crank-pin Z will revolve clockwise
   B. the crosshead Y will move in a direction opposite to that of X
   C. the crank-pin Z will revolve counterclockwise
   D. no movement will take place
   E. the crank-pin Z will oscillate back and forth

5. If we start from the position shown in the above diagram, and move piston X to the right, the result will be that 5____

   A. the crank-pin Z will revolve counterclockwise and cross-head Y will move to the left
   B. the crank-pin Z will revolve clockwise and crosshead Y will move to the left
   C. the crank-pin Z will revolve clockwise and crosshead Y will move to the right
   D. the crank-pin Z will revolve clockwise and crosshead Y will move to the right
   E. crosshead Y will move to the left as piston X moves to the right

6. If crank-pin Z is moved closer to the center of the crank circle, then the length of the 6____

   A. stroke of piston X is increased
   B. stroke of piston X is decreased
   C. stroke of piston X is unchanged
   D. rod between the piston X and crosshead Y is increased
   E. rod between the piston X and crosshead Y is decreased

Questions 7-8.

DIRECTIONS: Figure II represents schematically a block-and-fall tackle. The advantage derived from this machine is that the effect of the applied force is multiplied by the number of lines of rope directly supporting the load. The following two questions, numbered 7 and 8, are to be answered with reference to this figure.

7. Pull P is exerted on line T to raise the load L. The line in which the *LARGEST* strain is finally induced is line 7____

   A. T   B. U   C. V   D. X   E. Y

104

8. If the largest pull P that two men can apply to line T is 280 lbs., the MAXIMUM load L that they can raise without regard to frictional losses is, *most nearly*, _____ lbs.
    A. 1960
    B. 1680
    C. 1400
    D. 1260
    E. 1120

8_____

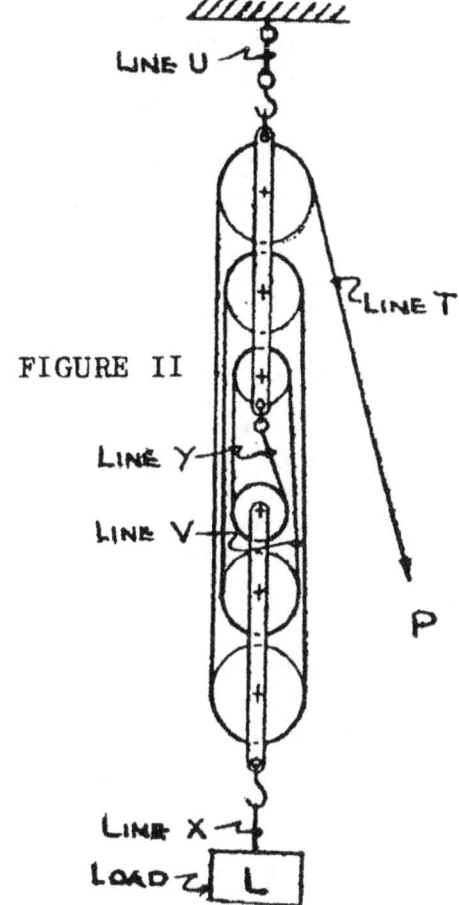

FIGURE II

Questions 9-13.

DIRECTIONS: Answer Questions 9 to 13 on the basis of Figure III. The diagram schematically illustrates part of a water tank. 1 and 5 are outlet and inlet pipes, respectively. 2 is a valve which can be used to open and close the outlet pipe by hand. 3 is a float which is rigidly connected to valve 4 by an iron bar, thus causing that valve to open or shut as the float rises or falls 4 is a hinged valve which controls the flow of water into the tank.

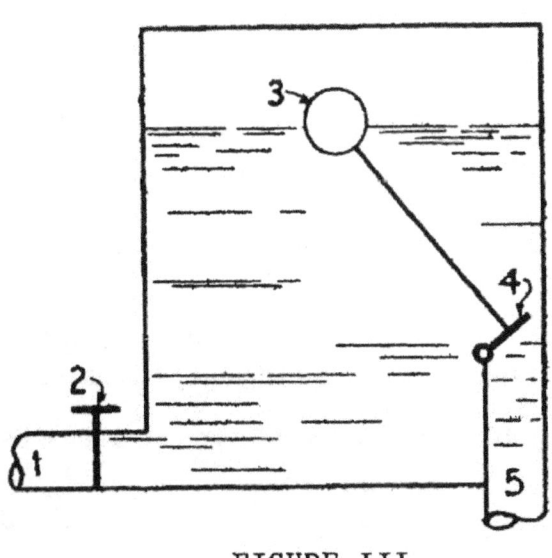

FIGURE III

4 (#3)

9. If the tank is half filled and water is going out of pipe 1 more rapidly than it is coming in through pipe 5, *then*

    A. valve 2 is closed
    B. float 3 is rising in the tank
    C. valve 4 is opening wider
    D. valve 4 is closed
    E. float 3 is stationary

10. If the tank is half filled with water and water is coming in through inlet pipe 5 more rapidly than it is going out through outlet pipe 1, *then*

    A. valve 2 is closed
    B. float 3 is rising in the tank
    C. valve 4 is opening wider
    D. valve 4 is closed
    E. float 3 is stationary

11. If the tank is empty, then it can *normally* be expected that

    A. float 3 is at its highest position
    B. float 3 is at its lowest position
    C. valve 2 is closed
    D. valve 4 is closed
    E. water will not come into the tank

12. If float 3 develops a leak, *then*

    A. the tank will tend to empty
    B. water will tend to stop coming into the tank
    C. valve 4 will tend to close
    D. valve 2 will tend to close
    E. valve 4 will tend to remain open

13. Without any other changes being made, if the bar joining the float to valve 4 is removed and a slightly shorter bar substituted, *then*

    A. a smaller quantity of water in the tank will be required before the float closes valve 4
    B. valve 4 will not open
    C. valve 4 will not close
    D. it is not possible to determine what will happen
    E. a greater quantity of water in the tank will be required before the float closes valve 4

Questions 14-18.

DIRECTIONS: Answer Questions 14 to 18 on the basis of Figure IV. A, B, C and D are four meshed gears forming a gear train. Gear A is the driver. Gears A and D each have twice as many teeth as gear B, and gear C has four times as many teeth as gear B. The diagram is schematic: the teeth go all around each gear.

14. *Two* gears which turn in the *same* direction are:

    A. A and B
    B. B and C
    C. C and D
    D. D and A
    E. B and D

15. The *two* gears which revolve at the *same* speed are gears

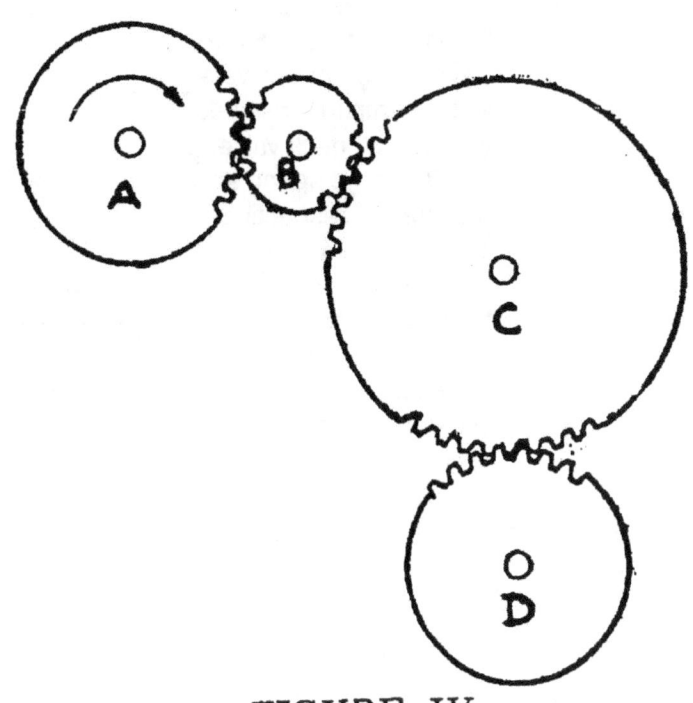

FIGURE IV

   A. A and C B. A and D C. B and C
   D. B and D E. D and C

16. If all the teeth on gear C are stripped without affecting the teeth on gears A, B, and D, then rotation would occur *only* in gear(s)

   A. C B. D C. A and B
   D. A, B, and D E. B and D

17. If gear D is rotating at the rate of 100 RPM, then gear B is rotating at the rate of _____ RPM.

   A. 25 B. 50 C. 100 D. 200 E. 400

18. If gear A turns at the rate of two revolutions per second, then the number of revolutions per second that gear C turns is

   A. 1 B. 2 C. 3 D. 4 E. 8

Questions 19-23.

DIRECTIONS: Answer Questions 19 to 23 on the basis of Figure V. The diagram shows a water pump in cross section: 1 is a check valve, 2 and 3 are the spring and diaphragm, respectively, of the discharge valve, 4 is the pump piston; 5 is the inlet valve, and 6 is the pump cylinder. All valves permit the flow of water in one direction only.

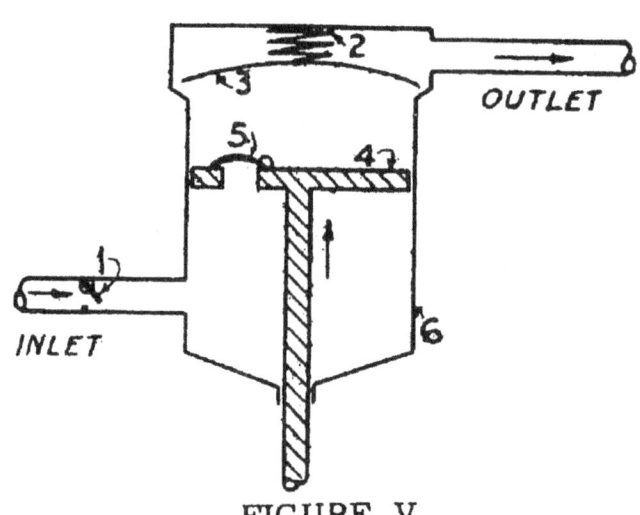

FIGURE V

19. When water is flowing through the outlet pipe,

    A. check valve 1 is closed
    B. diaphragm 3 is closed
    C. valve 5 is closed
    D. spring 2 is fully extended
    E. the piston is on the downstroke

20. If valve 5 does not work properly and stays closed, *then*

    A. the piston cannot move down
    B. the piston cannot move up
    C. diaphragm 3 cannot open
    D. check valve 1 cannot close
    E. the flow of water will be reversed

21. If diaphragm 3 does not work properly and stays in the open position, *then*

    A. check valve 1 will not open
    B. valve 5 will not open
    C. spring 2 will be compressed
    D. spring 2 will be extended
    E. water will not flow through the inlet pipe

22. When valve 5 is open during normal operation of the pump, *then*

    A. spring 2 is fully compressed
    B. the piston is on the upstroke
    C. water is flowing through check valve 1
    D. a vacuum is formed between the piston and the bottom of the cylinder
    E. diaphragm 3 is closed

23. If check valve 1 jams and stays closed, *then*

    A. valve 5 will be open on both the upstroke and down stroke of the piston
    B. a vacuum will tend to form in the inlet pipe between the source of the water supply and check valve 1
    C. pressure on the cylinder side of check valve 1 will increase

D. less force will be required to move the piston down
E. more force will be required to move the piston down

24. The one of the following which BEST explains why smoke usually rises from a fire is that   24____

    A. cooler, heavier air displaces lighter, warm air
    B. heat energy of the fire propels the smoke upward
    C. suction from the upper air pulls the smoke upward
    D. burning matter is chemically changed into heat energy

25. The practice of racing a car engine to warm it up in cold weather, generally, is   25____

    A. *good, MAINLY* because repeated stalling of the engine and drain on the battery is avoided
    B. *bad, MAINLY* because too much gas is used to get the engine heated
    C. *good, MAINLY* because the engine becomes operational in the shortest period of time
    D. *bad, MAINLY* because proper lubrication is not established rapidly enough

KEY (CORRECT ANSWERS)

1.	C	11.	B
2.	B	12.	E
3.	B	13.	A
4.	D	14.	E
5.	D	15.	B
6.	B	16.	C
7.	B	17.	D
8.	B	18.	A
9.	C	19.	C
10.	B	20.	A

21. C
22. E
23. D
24. A
25. D

ARITHMETICAL REASONING
EXAMINATION SECTION
TEST 1

DIRECTIONS: Each question or incomplete statement is followed by several suggested answers or completions. Select the one that BEST answers the question or completes the statement. *PRINT THE LETTER OF THE CORRECT ANSWER IN THE SPACE AT THE RIGHT.*

1.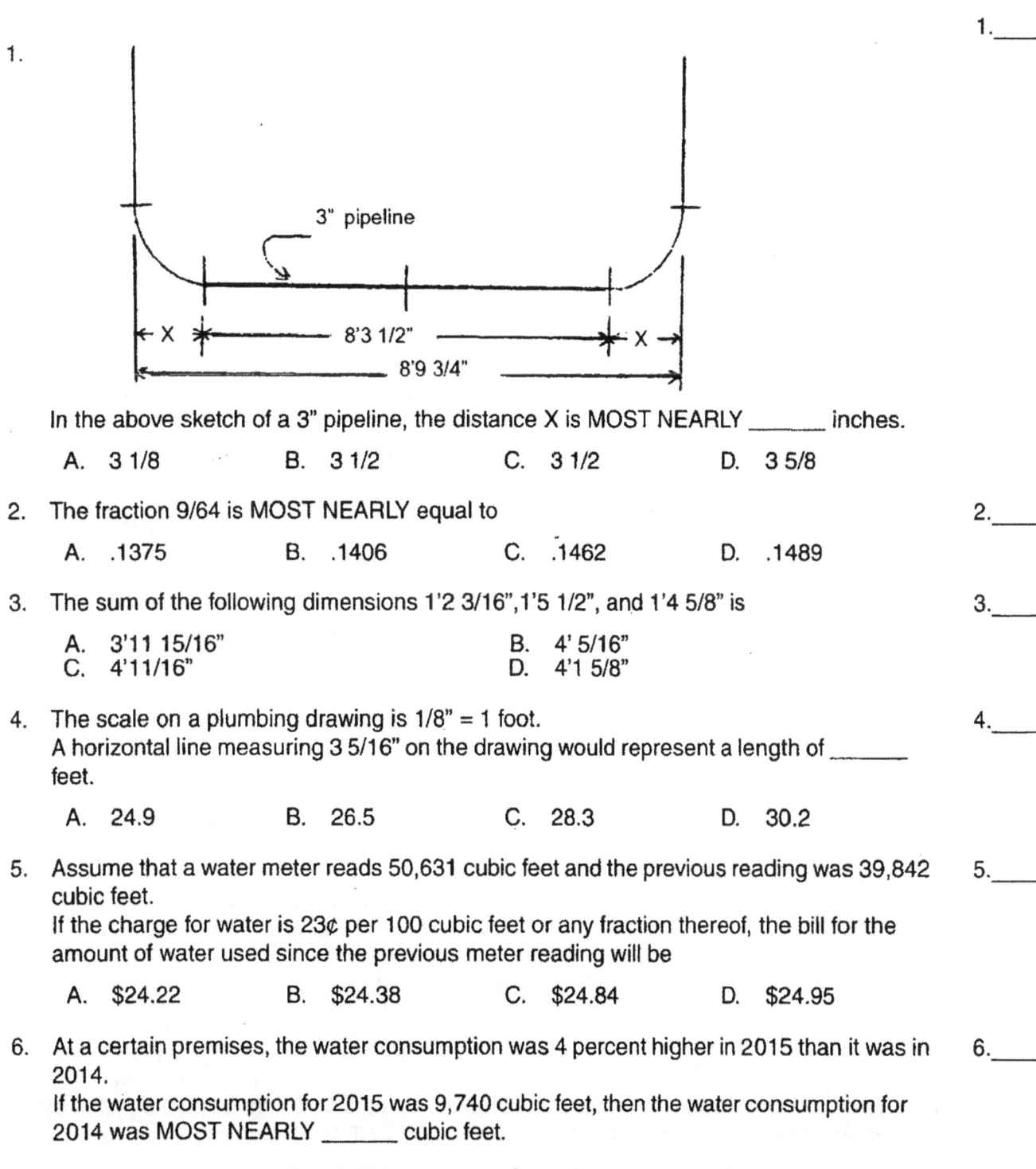

    In the above sketch of a 3" pipeline, the distance X is MOST NEARLY _____ inches.

    A. 3 1/8   B. 3 1/2   C. 3 1/2   D. 3 5/8

2. The fraction 9/64 is MOST NEARLY equal to

    A. .1375   B. .1406   C. .1462   D. .1489

3. The sum of the following dimensions 1'2 3/16", 1'5 1/2", and 1'4 5/8" is

    A. 3'11 15/16"   B. 4' 5/16"
    C. 4'11/16"   D. 4'1 5/8"

4. The scale on a plumbing drawing is 1/8" = 1 foot.
   A horizontal line measuring 3 5/16" on the drawing would represent a length of _____ feet.

    A. 24.9   B. 26.5   C. 28.3   D. 30.2

5. Assume that a water meter reads 50,631 cubic feet and the previous reading was 39,842 cubic feet.
   If the charge for water is 23¢ per 100 cubic feet or any fraction thereof, the bill for the amount of water used since the previous meter reading will be

    A. $24.22   B. $24.38   C. $24.84   D. $24.95

6. At a certain premises, the water consumption was 4 percent higher in 2015 than it was in 2014.
   If the water consumption for 2015 was 9,740 cubic feet, then the water consumption for 2014 was MOST NEARLY _____ cubic feet.

    A. 9,320   B. 9,350   C. 9,365   D. 9,390

7. A pump delivers water at a constant rate of 40 gallons per minute.
   If there are 7.5 gallons to a cubic foot of water, the time it will take to fill a tank 6 feet x 5 feet x 4 feet is MOST NEARLY _____ minutes.

   A. 15   B. 22.5   C. 28.5   D. 30

8. The total weight, in pounds, of three lengths of 3" cast-iron pipe 7'6" long, weighing 14.5 pounds per foot, and four lengths of 4" cast-iron pipe each 5'0" long, weighing 13.0 pounds per foot, is MOST NEARLY

   A. 540   B. 585   C. 600   D. 665

9. The water pressure at the bottom of a column of water 34 feet high is 14.7 lbs./sq.in. The water pressure in lbs./sq.in. at the bottom of the column of water 12 feet high is MOST NEARLY

   A. 3   B. 5   C. 7   D. 9

10. The number of cubic yards of earth that would be removed when digging a trench 8 feet wide x 9 feet deep x 63 feet long is

    A. 56   B. 168   C. 314   D. 504

11. On test, a meter registered one cubic foot for each 1 1/3 cubic feet of water that passed through it.
    If the meter had a reading of 1,200 cubic feet, we may conclude that the CORRECT amount should be _____ cubic feet.

    A. 800   B. 900   C. 1,500   D. 1,600

12. A water use meter reads 87,463 cubic feet.
    If the previous reading was 17,377 cubic feet and the rate charged is 15 cents per 100 cubic feet, the bill for water use during this period is about

    A. $45.00   B. $65.00   C. $85.00   D. $105.00

13. Under proper conditions, the one of the following groups of pipes that gives the same flow in gals/min as one 6" diameter pipe is (neglect friction) _____ pipes of _____ diameter each.

    A. 3; 3"   B. 4; 3"   C. 2; 4"   D. 3; 4"

14. A roof tank is used to furnish the domestic water supply to a ten story building. This tank has a capacity of 5,900 gallons. At 10:00 A.M. one morning, the tank is half full.
    If water is being used at the rate of 50 gals/min, the pump which is used to fill the tank has a rated capacity of 90 gals/min, the time it would take to fill the tank under these conditions is MOST NEARLY _____ hour(s), _____ minutes.

    A. 2; 8   B. 1; 14   C. 2; 32   D. 1; 2

15. The number of gallons of water contained in a cylindrical swimming pool 8 feet in diameter and filled to a depth of 3 feet 6 inches is MOST NEARLY (assume 7.5 gallons = 1 cubic foot)

    A. 30   B. 225   C. 1,320   D. 3,000

16. The charge for metered water is 52 1/2 cents per hundred cubic feet, with a minimum charge of $21 per annum. Of the following, the SMALLEST water usage in hundred cubic feet that would result in a charge GREATER than the minimum is

    A. 39　　B. 40　　C. 41　　D. 42

17. The annual frontage rent on a one-story building 40 ft. in length is $735.00. For each additional story, $52.50 per annum is added to the frontage rent. For demolition, the charge for wetting down is 3/8 of the annual frontage charge.
    The charge for wetting down a building six stories in height, with a 40 ft. frontage, is MOST NEARLY

    A. $369　　B. $371　　C. $372　　D. $374

18. If the drawing of a piping layout is made to a scale of 1/4" equals one foot, then a 7'9" length of piping would be represented by a scaled length on the drawing of APPROXIMATELY _____ inches.

    A. 2　　B. 7 3/4　　C. 23 1/4　　D. 31

19. A plumbing sketch is drawn to a scale of eighth-size. A line measuring 3" on the sketch would be equivalent to _____ feet.

    A. 2　　B. 6　　C. 12　　D. 24

20. If 500 feet of pipe weighs 800 lbs., the number of pounds that 120 feet will weigh is MOST NEARLY

    A. 190　　B. 210　　C. 230　　D. 240

21. If a trench is excavated 3'0" wide by 5'6" deep and 50 feet long, the total number of cubic yards of earth removed is MOST NEARLY

    A. 30　　B. 90　　C. 150　　D. 825

22. Assume that a plumber earns $86,500 per year.
    If eighteen percent of his pay is deducted for taxes and social security, his net weekly pay will be APPROXIMATELY

    A. $1,326　　B. $1,365　　C. $1,436　　D. $1,457.50

23. Assume that a plumbing installation is made up of the following fixtures and groups of fixtures: 12 bathroom groups each containing one W.C., one lavatory, and one bathtub with shower; 12 bathroom groups each containing one W.C., one lavatory, one bathtub, and one shower stall; 24 combination kitchen fixtures; 4 floor drains; 6 slop sinks without flushing rim; and 2 shower stalls (or shower bath).
    The total number of fixtures for the above plumbing installation is MOST NEARLY

    A. 60　　B. 95　　C. 120　　D. 210

24. A triangular opening in a wall forms a 30-60 degree right triangle.
    If the longest side measures 12'0", then the shortest side will measure

    A. 3'0"　　B. 4'0"　　C. 6'0"　　D. 8'0"

25. You are directed to cut 4 pieces of pipe, one each of the following length: 2'6 1/4", 3'9 3/8", 4'7 5/8", and 5'8 7/8".
The total length of these 4 pieces is

   A. 15'7 1/4"   B. 15'9 3/8"   C. 16'5 7/8"   D. 16'8 1/8"

25.____

KEY (CORRECT ANSWERS)

1.	A	11.	D
2.	B	12.	D
3.	B	13.	B
4.	B	14.	B
5.	C	15.	C
6.	C	16.	C
7.	B	17.	D
8.	B	18.	A
9.	B	19.	A
10.	B	20.	A

21. A
22. B
23. C
24. C
25. D

SOLUTIONS TO PROBLEMS

1. 8'3 1/2" + x + x = 8'9 3/4" Then, 2x = 6 1/4", so x = 3 1/8"

2. 9/64 = .140625 = .1406

3. 1'2 3/16" + 1'5 1/2" +1'4 5/8" = 3'11 21/16" = 4'5/16"

4. 3 5/16" ÷ 1/8" =53/16 x 8/1 = 26.5. Then, (26.5)(1 ft.) = 26.5 feet

5. 50,631 - 39,842 = 10,789; 10,789 ÷ 100 = 107.89
    Since the cost is .23 per 100 cubic feet or any fraction thereof, the cost will be
    (.23)(107) + .23 = $24.84

6. 9740 ÷ 1.04 = 9365 cu.ft.

7. 40 ÷ 7.5 = 5 1/3 cu.ft. of water per minute. The volume = (6)(5)(4) = 120 cu.ft. Thus, the number of minutes needed to fill the tank is 120 ÷ 5 1/3 = 22.5

8. 3" pipe: 3 x 7'6" = 22 1/2' x 14.5 lbs. = 326.25
    4" pipe: 4 x 5' = 20' x 13 lbs. = 260
    326.25 + 260 = 586.25 (most nearly 585)

9. Let x = pressure. Then, 34/12 = 14.7/x. So, 34x = 176.4
    Solving, x ≈ 5 lbs./sq.in.

10. (8)(9)(63) = 4536 cu.ft. Since 1 cu.yd. = 27 cu.ft., 4536 cu.ft. is equivalent to 168 cu.yds.

11. Let x = correct amount. Then, $\dfrac{1}{1200} = \dfrac{1\frac{1}{3}}{x}$. Solving, x = 1600

12. 87,463 - 17,377 = 70,086; and 70,086 ÷ 100 = 700.86 ≈ 700 Then, (700)(.15) = $105.00

13. Cross-sectional area of a 6" diameter pipe = (π)(3")^2 = 9π sq. in. Note that the combined cross-sectional areas of four 3" diameter pipes = (4)(π)(1.5")^2 = 9π sq. in.

14. 90 - 50 = 40 gals/min. Then, 2950 ÷ 40 = 73.75 min. ≈ 1 hr. 14 min.

15. Volume = (π)(4)^2(3 1/2) = 56π cu.ft. Then, (56π)(7.5) = 1320 gals.

16. For 4100 cu.ft., the charge of (.525)(41) = $21,525 > $21

17. Rent = $73,500 + (5)($52.50) = $997,50. For demolition, the charge = (3/8)($997.50)
    $374

18. (1/4")(7.75) = 2"

19. (3")(8) = 24" = 2 ft.

20. Let x = weight. Then, 500/800 = 120/x . Solving, x = 192 190 lbs.

21. (3')(5 1/2')(50') = 825 cu.ft. Then, 825 ÷ 27 ≈ 30 cu.yds.

22. Net pay = (.82)($86,500) = $70,930/yr. Weekly pay = $70,930 ÷ 52 ≈ $1365

23. (12x3) + (12x4) +24+4+6+2= 120

24. The shortest side = (1/2)(hypotenuse) = (1/2)(12') = 6'

25. 2'6 1/4" + 3'9 3/8" + 4'7 5/8" + 5'8 7/8 " = 14'30 17/8" = 16'8 1/8"

TEST 2

DIRECTIONS: Each question or incomplete statement is followed by several suggested answers or completions. Select the one that BEST answers the question or completes the statement. *PRINT THE LETTER OF THE CORRECT ANSWER IN THE SPACE AT THE RIGHT.*

1. The sum of the following pipe lengths, 15 5/8", 8 3/4", 30 5/16" and 20 1/2", is 1.____
    A. 77 1/8"   B. 76 3/16"   C. 75 3/16"   D. 74 5/16"

2. If the outside diameter of a pipe is 6 inches and the wall thickness is 1/2 inch, the inside area of this pipe, in square inches, is MOST NEARLY 2.____
    A. 15.7   B. 17.3   C. 19.6   D. 23.8

3. Three lengths of pipe 1'10", 3'2 1/2", and 5'7 1/2", respectively, are to be cut from a pipe 14'0" long. 3.____
   Allowing 1/8" for each pipe cut, the length of pipe remaining is
    A. 3'1 1/8"   B. 3'2 1/2"   C. 3'3 1/4"   D. 3'3 5/8"

4. According to the building code, the MAXIMUM permitted surface temperature of combustible construction materials located near heating equipment is 76.5°C. (°F=(°Cx9/5)+32) 4.____
   Maximum temperature Fahrenheit is MOST NEARLY
    A. 170° F   B. 195° F   C. 210° F   D. 220° F

5. A pump discharges 7.5 gals/minutes. 5.____
   In 2.5 hours the pump will discharge _____ gallons.
    A. 1125   B. 1875   C. 1950   D. 2200

6. A pipe with an outside diameter of 4" has a circumference of MOST NEARLY _____ inches. 6.____
    A. 8.05   B. 9.81   C. 12.57   D. 14.92

7. A piping sketch is drawn to a scale of 1/8" = 1 foot. 7.____
   A vertical steam line measuring 3 1/2" on the sketch would have an ACTUAL length of _____ feet.
    A. 16   B. 22   C. 24   D. 28

8. A pipe having an inside diameter of 3.48 inches and a wall thickness of .18 inches will have an outside diameter of _____ inches. 8.____
    A. 3.84   B. 3.64   C. 3.57   D. 3.51

9. A rectangular steel bar having a volume of 30 cubic inches, a width of 2 inches, and a height of 3 inches will have a length of _____ inches. 9.____
    A. 12   B. 10   C. 8   D. 5

10. A pipe weighs 20.4 pounds per foot of length. 10.____
    The total weight of eight pieces of this pipe with each piece 20 feet in length is MOST NEARLY _____ pounds.
     A. 460   B. 1,680   C. 2,420   D. 3,260

11. Assume that four pieces of pipe measuring 2'1 1/4", 4'2 3/4", 5'1 9/16", and 6'3 5/8", respectively, are cut with a saw from a pipe 20'0" long.
Allowing 1/16" waste for each cut, the length of the remaining pipe is

   A. 2'1 9/16"   B. 2'2 9/16"   C. 2'4 13/16"   D. 2'8 9/16"

12. If one cubic inch of steel weighs 0.28 pounds, the weight, in pounds, of a steel bar 1/2" x 6" x 2'0" long is MOST NEARLY

   A. 11   B. 16   C. 20   D. 24

13. If the circumference of a circle is equal to 31.416 inches, then its diameter, in inches, is equal to MOST NEARLY

   A. 8   B. 9   C. 10   D. 13

14. Assume that a steam fitter's helper receives a salary of $171.36 a day for 250 days is considered a full work year. If taxes, social security, hospitalization, and pension deducted from his salary amounts to 16 percent of his gross pay, then his net yearly salary will be MOST NEARLY

   A. $31,788   B. $35,982   C. $41,982   D. $42,840

15. If the outside diameter of a pipe is 14 inches and the wall thickness is 1/2 inch, then the inside area of the pipe, in square inches, is MOST NEARLY

   A. 125   B. 133   C. 143   D. 154

16. A steam leak in a pipe line allows steam to escape at a rate of 50,000 pounds each month.
Assuming that the cost of steam is $2.50 per 1,000 pounds, the TOTAL cost of wasted steam from this leak for a 12-month period would amount to

   A. $125   B. $300   C. $1,500   D. $3,000

17. If 250 feet of 4" pipe weighs 400 pounds, the weight of this pipe per linear foot is _____ pounds.

   A. 1.25   B. 1.50   C. 1.60   D. 1.75

18. A set of heating plan drawings is drawn to a scale of 1/4" = 1 foot.
If a length of pipe measures 4 5/8" on the drawing, the ACTUAL length of the pipe, in feet, is

   A. 16.3   B. 16.8   C. 17.5   D. 18.5

19. The TOTAL length of four pieces of pipe whose lengths are 3'4 1/2", 2'1 5/16", 4'9 3/8", and 2'3 1/4", respectively, is

   A. 11'5 7/16"   B. 11'6 7/16"
   C. 12'5 7/16"   D. 12'6 7/16"

20. Assume that a pipe trench is 3 feet wide, 3 feet deep, and 300 feet long.
If the unit cost of excavating the trench is $120 per cubic yard, the TOTAL cost of excavating the trench is

   A. $1,200   B. $12,000   C. $27,000   D. $36,000

21. The TOTAL length of four pieces of 1 1/2" galvanized steel pipe whose lengths are 7 ft. + 3 1/2 inches, 4 ft. + 2 1/4 inches, 6 ft. + 7 inches, and 8 ft. +5 1/8 inches is   21._____

    A. 26 feet + 5 7/8 inches B. 25 ft. + 6 7/8 inches
    C. 25 feet + 4 1/4 inches D. 25 ft. + 3 3/8 inches

22. A swimming pool is 25' wide by 75' long and has an average depth of 5'. 1 cubic foot contains 7.5 gallons of water. The capacity, when filled to the overflow, is _____ gallons.   22._____

    A. 9,375   B. 65,625   C. 69,005   D. 70,312

23. The sum of 3 1/4, 5 1/8, 2 1/2 , and 3 3/8 is   23._____

    A. 14   B. 14 1/8   C. 14 1/4   D. 14 3/8

24. Assume that it takes 6 men 8 days to do a particular job. If you have only 4 men available to do this job and they all work at the same speed, then the number of days it would take to complete the job would be   24._____

    A. 11   B. 12   C. 13   D. 14

25. The total length of four pieces of 2" O.D. pipe, whose lengths are 7'3 1/2", 4'2 3/16", 5'7 5/16", and 8'5 7/8", respectively, is MOST NEARLY   25._____

    A. 24'6 3/4"   B. 24'7 15/16"
    C. 25'5 13/16"   D. 25'6 7/8"

KEY (CORRECT ANSWERS)

1.	C	11.	B
2.	C	12.	C
3.	D	13.	C
4.	A	14.	B
5.	A	15.	B
6.	C	16.	C
7.	D	17.	C
8.	A	18.	D
9.	D	19.	D
10.	D	20.	B

21. A
22. D
23. C
24. B
25. D

/ 4 (#2)

SOLUTIONS TO PROBLEMS

1. 15 5/8" + 8 3/4" + 30 5/16" + 20 1/2" = 73 35/16" = 75 3/16"

2. Inside diameter = 6" - 1/2" - 1/2" = 5". Area = $(\pi)(5/2")^2 \approx$ 19.6 sq. in.

3. Pipe remaining = 14' - 1'10" - 3'2 1/2" - 5'7 1/2" - (3)(1/8") = 3'3 5/8"

4. 76.5 x 9/5 = 137.7 + 32 = 169.7

5. 7.5 x 150 = 1125

6. Radius = 2" Circumference = $(2\pi)(2") \approx$ 12.57"

7. 3 1/2" 1/8" = (7/2)(8/1) = 28 Then, (28)(1 ft.) = 28 feet

8. Outside diameter = 3.48" + .18" + .18" = 3.84"

9. 30 = (2)(3)(length). So, length = 5"

10. Total weight = (20.4)(8)(20) $\approx$ 3260 lbs.

11. 20' - 2'1 1/4" - 4'2 3/4" - 5'1 9/16" - 6'3 5/8" - (4)(1/16") = 2'2 9/16"

12. Weight = (.28)(1/2")(6")(24") = 20.16 $\approx$ 20 lbs.

13. Diameter = 31.416" ÷ $\pi \approx$ 10"

14. His net pay for 250 days = (.84)($171.36)(250) = $35,985.60 $\approx$ $35,928 (from answer key)

15. Inside diameter = 14" - 1/2" - 1/2" = 13". Area = $(\pi)(13/2")^2 \approx$ 133 sq.in

16. (50,000 lbs.)(12) = 600,000 lbs. per year. The cost would be ($2.50)(600) = $1500

17. 400 ÷ 250 = 1.60 pounds per linear foot

18. 4 5/8" ÷ 1/4" = 37/8 . 4/1 = 18.5 Then, (18.5)(1 ft.) = 18.5 feet

19. 3'4 1/2" + 2'1 5/16" + 4'9 3/8" + 2'3 1/4" = 11'17 23/16" = 12'6 7/16"

20. (3')(3')(300') = 2700 cu.ft., which is 2700 ÷ 27 = 100 cu.yds. Total cost = ($120)(100) = $12,000

21. 7'3 1/2" + 4'2 1/4" + 6'7" + 8'5 1/8" = 25'17 7/8" = 26'5 7/8"

22. (25)(75)(5) = 9375 cu.ft. Then, (9375)(7.5) $\approx$ 70,312 gals.

23. 3 1/4 + 5 1/8 + 2 1/2 + 3 3/8 = 13 10/8 = 14 1/4

24. (6) (8) = 48 man-days. Then, 48 ÷ 4 = 12 days

25. 7'3 1/2" + 4'2 3/16" + 5'7 5/16" + 8'5 7/8"= 24'17 30/16" = 25'6 7/8"

TEST 3

DIRECTIONS: Each question or incomplete statement is followed by several suggested answers or completions. Select the one that BEST answers the question or completes the statement. *PRINT THE LETTER OF THE CORRECT ANSWER IN THE SPACE AT THE RIGHT.*

1. The time required to pump 2,500 gallons of water out of a sump at the rate of 12 1/2 gallons per minutes would be _____ hour(s) _____ minutes.   1.____

    A. 1; 40   B. 2; 30   C. 3; 20   D. 6; 40

2. Copper tubing which has an inside diameter of 1 1/16" and a wall thickness of .095" has an outside diameter which is MOST NEARLY _____ inches.   2.____

    A. 1 5/32   B. 1 3/16   C. 1 7/32   D. 1 1/4

3. Assume that 90 gallons per minute flow through a certain 3-inch pipe which is tapped into a street main.   3.____
The amount of water which would flow through a 1-inch pipe tapped into the same street main is MOST NEARLY _____ gpm.

    A. 90   B. 45   C. 30   D. 10

4. The weight of a 6 foot length of 8-inch pipe which weighs 24.70 pounds per foot is _____ lbs.   4.____

    A. 148.2   B. 176.8   C. 197.6   D. 212.4

5. If a 4-inch pipe is directly coupled to a 2-inch pipe and 16 gallons per minute are flowing through the 4-inch pipe, then the flow through the 2-inch pipe will be _____ gallons per minute.   5.____

    A. 4   B. 8   C. 16   D. 32

6. If the water pressure at the bottom of a column of water 34 feet high is 14.7 pounds per square inch, the water pressure at the bottom of a column of water 18 feet high is MOST NEARLY _____ pounds per square inch.   6.____

    A. 8.0   B. 7.8   C. 7.6   D. 7.4

7. If there are 7 1/2 gallons in a cubic foot of water and if water flows from a hose at a constant rate of 4 gallons per minute, the time it should take to COMPLETELY fill a tank of 1,600 cubic feet capacity with water from that hose is _____ hours.   7.____

    A. 300   B. 150   C. 100   D. 50

8. Each of a group of fifteen water meter readers read an average of 62 water meters a day in a certain 5-day work week. A total of 5,115 meters are read by this group the following week.   8.____
The TOTAL number of meters read in the second week as compared to the first week shows a

    A. 10% increase   B. 15% increase
    C. 20% increase   D. 5% decrease

121

9. A certain water consumer used 5% more water in 1994 than he did in 1993.
If his water consumption for 1994 was 8,375 cubic feet, the amount of water he consumed in 1993 was MOST NEARLY _____ cubic feet.

   A. 9,014 B. 8,816 C. 7,976 D. 6,776

10. Assume that a water meter reads 40,175 cubic feet and that the previous reading was 29,186 cubic feet.
If the charge for water is 92 cents per 100 cubic feet or any fraction thereof, the bill for the amount of water used since the previous meter reading should be

    A. $100.28 B. $101.04 C. $101.08 D. $101.20

11. A leaking faucet caused a loss of 216 cubic feet of water in a 30-day month.
If there are 7.5 gallons in a cubic foot of water, then the AVERAGE loss of water per hour for that month was _____ gallons.

    A. 2 1/4 B. 2 1/8 C. 2 D. 1 3/4

12. The fraction which is equal to .375 is

    A. 3/16 B. 5/32 C. 3/8 D. 5/12

13. A square backyard swimming pool, each side of which is 10 feet long, is filled to a depth of 3 1/2 feet.
If there are 7 1/2 gallons in a cubic foot of water, the number of gallons of water in the pool is MOST NEARLY _____ gallons.

    A. 46.7 B. 100 C. 2,625 D. 3,500

14. When 1 5/8, 3 3/4, 6 1/3, and 9 1/2 are added, the resulting sum is

    A. 21 1/8 B. 21 1/6 C. 21 5/24 D. 21 1/4

15. When 946 1/2 is subtracted from 1,035 1/4, the result is

    A. 87 1/4 B. 87 3/4 C. 88 1/4 D. 88 3/4

16. When 39 is multiplied by 697, the result is

    A. 8,364 B. 26,283 C. 27,183 D. 28,003

17. When 16.074 is divided by .045, the result is

    A. 3.6 B. 35.7 C. 357.2 D. 3,572

18. To dig a trench 3'0" wide, 50'0" long, and 5'6" deep, the total number of cubic yards of earth to be removed is MOST NEARLY

    A. 30 B. 90 C. 140 D. 825

19. The TOTAL length of four pieces of 2" pipe, whose lengths are 7'3 1/2", 4'2 3/16", 5'7 5/16", and 8'5 7/8", respectively, is

    A. 24'6 3/4" B. 24'7 15/16"
    C. 25'5 13/16" D. 25'6 7/8"

20. A hot water line made of copper has a straight horizontal run of 150 feet and, when installed, is at a temperature of 45° F. In use, its temperature rises to 190° F.
If the coefficient of expansion for copper is 0.0000095" per foot per degree F, the TOTAL expansion, in inches, in the run of pipe is given by the product of 150 multiplied by 0.0000095 by

    A. 145
    B. 145 x 12
    C. 145 divided by 12
    D. 145 x 12 x 12

21. A water storage tank measures 5' long, 4' wide, and 6' deep and is filled to the 5 1/2' mark with water.
If one cubic foot of water weighs 62 pounds, the number of pounds of water required to COMPLETELY fill the tank is

    A. 7,440   B. 6,200   C. 1,240   D. 620

22. Assume that a pipe worker earns $83,125.00 per year.
If seventeen percent of his pay is deducted for taxes, social security, and pension, his net weekly pay will be APPROXIMATELY

    A. $1598.50   B. $1504.00   C. $1453.00   D. $1325.00

23. If eighteen feet of 4" cast iron pipe weighs approximately 390 pounds, the weight of this pipe per lineal foot will be MOST NEARLY _____ lbs.

    A. 19   B. 22   C. 23   D. 25

24. If it takes 3 men 11 days to dig a trench, the number of days it will take 5 men to dig the same trench, assuming all work is done at the same rate of speed, is MOST NEARLY

    A. 6 1/2   B. 7 3/4   C. 8 1/4   D. 8 3/4

25. If a trench is dug 6'0" deep, 2'6" wide, and 8'0" long, the area of the opening, in square feet, is MOST NEARLY

    A. 48   B. 32   C. 20   D. 15

KEY (CORRECT ANSWERS)

1. C
2. D
3. D
4. A
5. B

6. B
7. D
8. A
9. C
10. D

11. A
12. C
13. C
14. C
15. D

16. C
17. C
18. A
19. D
20. A

21. D
22. D
23. B
24. A
25. C

SOLUTIONS TO PROBLEMS

1. 2500 ÷ 12 1/2 = 200 min. = 3 hrs. 20 min.

2. 1 1/16" + .095" + .095" = 1.0625 + .095 + .095 = 1.2525" ≈ 1 1/4"

3. Cross-sectional areas for a 3-inch pipe and a 1-inch pipe are $(\pi)(1.5)^2$ and $(\pi)(.5)^2$ = 2.25π and $.25\pi$, respectively. Let x = amount of water flowing through the 1-inch pipe. Then, $\frac{90}{x} = \frac{2.25\pi}{.25\pi}$. Solving, x = 10 gals/min

4. (24.70)(6) = 148.2 lbs.

5. $\frac{4" \text{ pipe}}{16 \text{ gallons}} = \frac{2" \text{ pipe}}{x \text{ gallons}}$, 4x = 32, x = 8

6. Let x = pressure. Then, 34/18 = 14.7/x. Solving, x ≈ 7.8

7. (1600)(7.5) = 12,000 gallons. Then, 12,000 ÷ 4 = 3000 min. = 50 hours

8. (15)(62)(5) = 4650. Then, (5115-4650)/4650 = 10% increase

9. 8375 ÷ 1.05 ≈ 7976 cu.ft.

10. 40,175 - 29,186 = 10,989 cu.ft. Then, 10,989 100 = 109.89. Since .92 is charged for each 100 cu.ft. or fraction thereof, total cost = (.92)(110) = $101.20

11. (216)(7.5) = 1620 gallons. In 30 days, there are 720 hours. Thus, the average water loss per hour = 1620 ÷ 720 = 2 1/4 gallons.

12. .375 = 375/1000 = 3/8

13. Volume = (10)(10)(3 1/2) = 350 cu.ft. Then, (350)(7 1/2) = 2625 gallons

14. 1 5/8 + 3 3/4 + 6 1/3 + 9 1/2 = 19 53/24 = 21 5/24

15. 1035 1/4 - 946 1/2 = 88 3/4

16. (39)(697) = 27,183

17. 16.074 .045 = 357.2

18. (3')(50')(5 1/2') = 825 cu.ft. ≈ 30 cu.yds., since 1 cu.yd. = 27 cu.ft.

19. 7'3 1/2" + 4'2 3/16" + 5'7 5/16" + 8'5 7/8" = 24'17 30/16" = 25'6 7/8"

20. Total expansion = (150)(.0000095)(145)

21. Number of pounds needed = (5)(4)(6-5 1/2)(62) = 620

22. Net annual pay = ($83,125)(.83) ≈ $69000. Then, the net weekly pay = $69000 ÷ 52 ≈ $1325 (actually about $1327)

23. 390 lbs. ÷ 18 = 21.6 lbs. per linear foot

24. (3)(11) = 33 man-days. Then, 33 ÷ 5 = 6.6 ≈ 6 1/2 days

25. Area = (8')(2 1/2') = 20 sq.ft.

EXAMINATION SECTION
TEST 1

DIRECTIONS: Each question or incomplete statement is followed by several suggested answers or completions. Select the one that BEST answers the question or completes the statement. *PRINT THE LETTER OF THE CORRECT ANSWER IN THE SPACE AT THE RIGHT.*

1. Which of the following is the MOST likely action a supervisor should take to help establish an effective working relationship with his departmental superiors?
    A. Delay the implementation of new procedures received from superiors in order to evaluate their appropriateness.
    B. Skip the chain of command whenever he feels that it is to his advantage
    C. Keep supervisors informed of problems in his area and the steps taken to correct them
    D. Don't take up superiors' time by discussing anticipated problems but wait until the difficulties occur

1.____

2. Of the following, the action a supervisor could take which would generally be MOST conducive to the establishment of an effective working relationship with employees includes
    A. maintaining impersonal relationships to prevent development of biased actions
    B. treating all employees equally without adjusting for individual differences
    C. continuous observation of employees on the job with insistence on constant improvement
    D. careful planning and scheduling of work for your employees

2.____

3. Which of the following procedures is the LEAST likely to establish effective working relationships between employees and supervisors?
    A. Encouraging two-way communication with employees
    B. Periodic discussion with employees regarding their job performance
    C. Ignoring employees' gripes concerning job difficulties
    D. Avoiding personal prejudices in dealing with employees

3.____

4. Criticism can be used as a tool to point out the weak areas of a subordinate's work performance.
   Of the following, the BEST action for a supervisor to take so that his criticism will be accepted is to
    A. focus his criticism on the act instead of on the person
    B. exaggerate the errors in order to motivate the employee to do better
    C. pass judgment quickly and privately without investigating the circumstances of the error
    D. generalize the criticism and not specifically point out the errors in performance

4.____

5. In trying to improve the motivation of his subordinates, a supervisor can achieve the BEST results by taking action based upon the assumption that most employees
   A. have an inherent dislike of work
   B. wish to be closely directed
   C. are more interested in security than in assuming responsibility
   D. will exercise self-direction without coercion

6. When there are conflicts or tensions between top management and lower-level employees in any department, the supervisor should FIRST attempt to
   A. represent and enforce the management point of view
   B. act as the representative of the workers to get their ideas across to management
   C. serve as a two-way spokesman, trying to interpret each side to the other
   D. remain neutral, but keep informed of changes in the situation

7. A probationary period for new employees is usually provided in many agencies. The MAJOR purpose of such a period is usually to
   A. allow a determination of employee's suitability for the position
   B. obtain evidence as to employee's ability to perform in a higher position
   C. conform to requirements that ethnic hiring goals be met for all positions
   D. train the new employee in the duties of the position

8. An effective program of orientation for new employees usually includes all of the following EXCEPT
   A. having the supervisor introduce the new employee to his job, outlining his responsibilities and how to carry them out
   B. permitting the new worker to tour the facility or department so he can observe all parts of it in action
   C. scheduling meetings for new employees, at which the job requirements are explained to them and they are given personnel manuals
   D. testing the new worker on his skills and sending him to a centralized in-service workshop

9. In-service training is an important responsibility of many supervisors. The MAJOR reason for such training is to
   A. avoid future grievance procedures because employees might say they were not prepared to carry out their jobs
   B. maximize the effectiveness of the department by helping each employee perform at his full potential
   C. satisfy inspection teams from central headquarters of the department
   D. help prevent disagreements with members of the community

10. There are many forms of useful in-service training.
    Of the following, the training method which is NOT an appropriate technique for leadership development is to
    A. provide special workshops or clinics in activity skills
    B. conduct institutes to familiarize new workers with the program of the department and with their roles

C. schedule team meetings for problem-solving, including both supervisors and leaders
D. have the leader rate himself on an evaluation form periodically

11. Of the following techniques of evaluating work training programs, the one that is BEST is to
    A. pass out a carefully designed questionnaire to the trainees at the completion of the program
    B. test the knowledge that trainees have both at the beginning of training and at its completion
    C. interview the trainees at the completion of the program
    D. evaluate performance before and after training for both a control group and an experimental group

11.____

12. Assume that a new supervisor is having difficulty making his instructions to subordinates clearly understood.
    The one of the following which is the FIRST step he should take in dealing with this problem is to
    A. set up a training workshop in communication skills
    B. determine the extent and nature of the communications gap
    C. repeat both verbal and written instructions several times
    D. simplify his written and spoken vocabulary

12.____

13. A director has not properly carried out the orders of his assistant supervisor on several occasions to the point where he has been successively warned, reprimanded, and severely reprimanded.
    When the director once again does not carry out orders, the PROPER action for the assistant supervisor to take is to
    A. bring the director up on charges of failing to perform his duties properly
    B. have a serious discussion with the director, explaining the need for the orders and the necessity for carrying them out
    C. recommend that the director be transferred to another district
    D. severely reprimand the director again, making clear that no further deviation will be countenanced

13.____

14. A supervisor with several subordinates becomes aware that two of these subordinates are neither friendly nor congenial.
    In making assignments, it would be BEST for the supervisor to
    A. disregard the situation
    B. disregard the situation in making a choice of assignment but emphasize the need for teamwork
    C. investigate the situation to find out who is at fault and give that individual the less desirable assignments until such time as he corrects his attitude
    D. place the unfriendly subordinates in positions where they have as little contact with one another as possible

14.____

15. A DESIRABLE characteristic of a good supervisor is that he should
    A. identify himself with his subordinates rather than with higher management
    B. inform subordinates of forthcoming changes in policies and programs only when they directly affect the subordinates' activities
    C. make advancement of the subordinates contingent on personal loyalty to the supervisor
    D. make promises to subordinates only when sure of the ability to keep them

16. The supervisor who is MOST likely to be successful is the one who
    A. refrains from exercising the special privileges of his position
    B. maintains a formal attitude toward his subordinates
    C. maintains an informal attitude toward his subordinates
    D. represents the desires of his subordinate to his superiors

17. Application of sound principles of human relations by a supervisor may be expected to _____ the need for formal discipline.
    A. decrease
    B. have no effect on
    C. increase
    D. obviate

18. The MOST important generally approved way to maintain or develop high morale in one's subordinates is to
    A. give warnings and reprimands in a jocular way
    B. excuse from staff conferences those employees who are busy
    C. keep them informed of new developments and policies of higher management
    D. refrain from criticizing their faults directly

19. In training subordinates, an IMPORTANT principle for the supervisor to recognize is that
    A. a particular method of instruction will be of substantially equal value for all employees in a given title
    B. it is difficult to train people over 50 years of age because they have little capacity for learning
    C. persons undergoing the same course of training will learn at different rates of speed
    D. training can seldom achieve its purpose unless individual instruction is the chief method used

20. Over an extended period of time, a subordinate is MOST likely to become and remain most productive if the supervisor
    A. accords praise to the subordinate whenever his work is satisfactory, withholding criticism except in the case of very inferior work
    B. avoids both praise and criticism except for outstandingly good or bad work performed by the subordinate
    C. informs the subordinate of his shortcomings, as viewed by management, while according praise only when highly deserved
    D. keeps the subordinate informed of the degree of satisfaction with which his performance of the job is viewed by management.

KEY (CORRECT ANSWERS)

1.	C	11.	D
2.	D	12.	B
3.	C	13.	A
4.	A	14.	D
5.	D	15.	D
6.	C	16.	D
7.	A	17.	A
8.	D	18.	C
9.	B	19.	C
10.	D	20.	D

TEST 2

DIRECTIONS: Each question or incomplete statement is followed by several suggested answers or completions. Select the one that BEST answers the question or completes the statement. *PRINT THE LETTER OF THE CORRECT ANSWER IN THE SPACE AT THE RIGHT.*

1. A supervisor has just been told by a subordinate, Mr. Jones, that another employee, Mr. Smith, deliberately disobeyed an important rule of the department by taking home some confidential departmental material.
   Of the following courses of action, it would be MOST advisable for the supervisor FIRST to
   A. discuss the matter privately with both Mr. Jones and Mrs. Smith at the same time
   B. call a meeting of the entire staff and discuss the matter generally without mentioning any employee by name
   C. arrange to supervise Mr. Smith's activities more closely
   D. discuss the matter privately with Mr. Smith

   1.____

2. The one of the following actions which would be MOST efficient and economical for a supervisor to take to minimize the effect of periodical fluctuations in the workload of his unit is to
   A. increase his permanent staff until it is large enough to handle the work of the busy loads
   B. request the purchase of time- and labor-saving equipment to be used primarily during the busy loads
   C. lower, temporarily, the standards for quality of work performance during peak loads
   D. schedule for the slow periods work that is not essential to perform during the busy periods

   2.____

3. Discipline of employees is usually a supervisor's responsibility. There may be several useful forms of disciplinary action.
   Of the following, the form that is LEAST appropriate is the
   A. written reprimand or warning
   B. involuntary transfer to another work setting
   C. demotion or suspension
   D. assignment of added hours of work each week

   3.____

4. Of the following, the MOST effective means of dealing with employee disciplinary problems is to
   A. give personality tests to individuals to identify their psychological problems
   B. distribute and discuss a policy manual containing exact rules governing employee behavior
   C. establish a single, clear penalty to be imposed for all wrongdoing irrespective of degree
   D. have supervisors get to know employees well through social mingling

   4.____

2 (#2)

5. A recently developed technique for appraising work performance is to have the supervisor record on a continual basis all significant incidents in each subordinate's behavior that indicate unsuccessful action and those that indicate poor behavior.
Of the following, a MAJOR disadvantage of this method of performance appraisal is that it
   A. often leads to overly close supervision
   B. results in competition among those subordinates being evaluated
   C. tends to result in superficial judgments
   D. lacks objectivity for evaluating performance

5.____

6. Assume that you are a supervisor and have observed the performance of an employee during a period of time. You have concluded that his performance needs improvement.
In order to improve his performance, it would, therefore, be BEST for you to
   A. note your findings in the employee's personnel folder so that his behavior is a matter of record
   B. report the findings to the personnel officer so he can take prompt action
   C. schedule a problem-solving conference with the employee
   D. recommend his transfer to simpler duties

6.____

7. When an employee's absences or latenesses seem to be nearing excessiveness, the supervisor should speak with him to find out what the problem is.
Of the following, if such a discussion produces no reasonable explanation, the discussion usually BEST serves to
   A. affirm clearly the supervisor's adherence to proper policy
   B. alert other employees that such behavior is unacceptable
   C. demonstrate that the supervisor truly represents higher management
   D. notify the employee that his behavior is being observed and evaluated

7.____

8. Assume that an employee willfully and recklessly violates an important agency regulation. The nature of the violation is of such magnitude that it demands immediate action, but the facts of the case are not entirely clear. Further, assume that the supervisor is free to make any of the following recommendations.
The MOST appropriate action for the supervisor to take is to recommend that the employee be
   A. discharged   B. suspended
   C. forced to resign   D. transferred

8.____

9. Although employees' titles may be identical, each position in that title may be considerably different.
Of the following, a supervisor should carefully assign each employee to a specific position based PRIMARILY on the employee's
   A. capability   B. experience   C. education   D. seniority

9.____

10. The one of the following situations where it is MOST appropriate to transfer an employee to a similar assignment is one in which the employee
    A. lacks motivation and interest
    B. experiences a personality conflict with his supervisor
    C. is negligent in the performance of his duties
    D. lacks capacity or ability to perform assigned tasks

10._____

11. The one of the following which is LEAST likely to be affected by improvements in the morale of personnel is employee
    A. skill
    B. absenteeism
    C. turnover
    D. job satisfaction

11._____

12. The one of the following situations in which it is LEAST appropriate for a supervisor to delegate authority to subordinates is where the supervisor
    A. lacks confidence in his own abilities to perform certain work
    B. is overburdened and cannot handle all his responsibilities
    C. refers all disciplinary problems to his subordinate
    D. has to deal with an emergency or crisis

12._____

13. Assume that it has come to your attention that two of your subordinates have shouted at each other and have almost engaged in a fist fight. Luckily, they were separated by some of the other employees.
    Of the following, your BEST immediate course of action would generally be to
    A. reprimand the senior of the two subordinates since he should have known better
    B. hear the story from both employees and any witnesses and then take needed disciplinary action
    C. ignore the matter since nobody was physically hurt
    D. immediately suspend and fine both employees pending a departmental hearing

13._____

14. You have been delegating some of your authority to one of your subordinates because of his leadership potential.
    Which of the following actions is LEAST conducive to the growth and development of this individual for a supervisory position?
    A. Use praise only when it will be effective
    B. Give very detailed instructions and supervise the employee closely to be sure that the instructions ae followed precisely
    C. Let the subordinate proceed with his planned course of action even if mistakes, within a permissible range, are made
    D. Intervene on behalf of the subordinate whenever an assignment becomes difficult for him

14._____

15. A rumor has been spreading in your department concerning the possibility of layoffs due to decreased revenues.
    As a supervisor, you should GENERALLY
    A. deny the rumor, whether it is true or false, in order to keep morale from declining

15._____

B. inform the men to the best of your knowledge about this situation and keep them advised of any new information
C. tell the men to forget about the rumor and concentrate on increasing their productivity
D. ignore the rumor since it is not authorized information

16. Within an organization, every supervisor should know to whom he reports and who reports to him.
The one of the following which is achieved by use of such structured relationships is
    A. unity of command
    B. confidentiality
    C. esprit de corps
    D. promotion opportunities

16.____

17. Almost every afternoon, one of your employees comes back from his break ten minutes late without giving you any explanation.
Which of the following actions should you take FIRST in this situation?
    A. Assign the employee to a different type of work and observe whether his behavior changes
    B. Give the employee extra work to do so that he will have to return on time
    C. Ask the employee for an explanation for his lateness
    D. Tell the employee he is jeopardizing the break for everyone

17.____

18. When giving instructions to your employees in a group, which one of the following should you make certain to do?
    A. Speak in a casual, off-hand manner
    B. Assume that your employees fully understand the instructions
    C. Write out your instructions beforehand and read them to the employees
    D. Tell exactly who is to do what

18.____

19. A fist fight develops between two men under your supervision.
The MOST advisable course of action for you to take FIRST is to
    A. call the police
    B. have the other workers pull them apart
    C. order them to stop
    D. step between the two men

19.____

20. You have assigned some difficult and unusual work to one of your most experienced and competent subordinates.
If you notice that he is doing the work incorrectly, you should
    A. assign the work to another employee
    B. reprimand him in private
    C. show him immediately how the work should be done
    D. wait until the job is completed and then correct his errors

20.____

KEY (CORRECT ANSWERS)

1.	D	11.	A
2.	D	12.	C
3.	D	13.	B
4.	B	14.	B
5.	A	15.	B
6.	C	16.	A
7.	D	17.	C
8.	B	18.	D
9.	A	19.	C
10.	B	20.	C

PHILOSOPHY, PRINCIPLES, PRACTICES, AND TECHNICS
OF
SUPERVISION, ADMINISTRATION, MANAGEMENT, AND ORGANIZATION

TABLE OF CONTENTS

	Page
MEANING OF SUPERVISION	1
THE OLD AND THE NEW SUPERVISION	1
THE EIGHT (8) BASIC PRINCIPLES OF THE NEW SUPERVISION	1
I. Principle of Responsibility	1
II. Principle of Authority	2
III. Principle of Self-Growth	2
IV. Principle of Individual Worth	2
V. Principle of Creative Leadership	2
VI. Principle of Success and Failure	2
VII. Principle of Science	3
VIII. Principle of Cooperation	3
WHAT IS ADMINISTRATION?	3
I. Practices Commonly Classed as "Supervisory"	3
II. Practices Commonly Classed as "Administrative"	3
III. Practices Commonly Classed as Both "Supervisory" and "Administrative"	4
RESPONSIBILITIES OF THE SUPERVISOR	4
COMPETENCIES OF THE SUPERVISOR	4
THE PROFESSIONAL SUPERVISOR-EMPLOYEE RELATIONSHIP	4
MINI-TEXT IN SUPERVISION, ADMINISTRATION, MANAGEMENT, AND ORGANIZATION	5
I. Brief Highlights	5
A. Levels of Management	6
B. What the Supervisor Must Learn	6
C. A Definition of Supervision	6
D. Elements of the Team Concept	6
E. Principles of Organization	6
F. The Four Important Parts of Every Job	7
G. Principles of Delegation	7
H. Principles of Effective Communications	7
I. Principles of Work Improvement	7
J. Areas of Job Improvement	7
K. Seven Key Points in Making Improvements	8

	L.	Corrective Techniques for Job Improvement	8
	M.	A Planning Checklist	8
	N.	Five Characteristics of Good Directions	9
	O.	Types of Directions	9
	P.	Controls	9
	Q.	Orienting the New Employee	9
	R.	Checklist for Orienting New Employees	9
	S.	Principles of Learning	10
	T.	Causes of Poor Performance	10
	U.	Four Major Steps in On-the-Job Instructions	10
	V.	Employees Want Five Things	10
	W.	Some Don'ts in Regard to Praise	11
	X.	How to Gain Your Workers' Confidence	11
	Y.	Sources of Employee Problems	11
	Z.	The Supervisor's Key to Discipline	11
	AA.	Five Important Processes of Management	12
	BB.	When the Supervisor Fails to Plan	12
	CC.	Fourteen General Principles of Management	12
	DD.	Change	12
II.	Brief Topical Summaries		13
	A.	Who/What is the Supervisor?	13
	B.	The Sociology of Work	13
	C.	Principles and Practices of Supervision	14
	D.	Dynamic Leadership	14
	E.	Processes for Solving Problems	15
	F.	Training for Results	15
	G.	Health, Safety, and Accident Prevention	16
	H.	Equal Employment Opportunity	16
	I.	Improving Communications	16
	J.	Self-Development	17
	K.	Teaching and Training	17
		1. The Teaching Process	17
		a. Preparation	17
		b. Presentation	18
		c. Summary	18
		d. Application	18
		e. Evaluation	18
		2. Teaching Methods	18
		a. Lecture	18
		b. Discussion	18
		c. Demonstration	19
		d. Performance	19
		e. Which Method to Use	19

PHILOSOPHY, PRINCIPLES, PRACTICES, AND TECHNICS
OF
SUPERVISION, ADMINISTRATION, MANAGEMENT, AND ORGANIZATION

MEANING OF SUPERVISION

The extension of the democratic philosophy has been accompanied by an extension in the scope of supervision. Modern leaders and supervisors no longer think of supervision in the narrow sense of being confined chiefly to visiting employees, supplying materials, or rating the staff. They regard supervision as being intimately related to all the concerned agencies of society, they speak of the supervisor's function in terms of "growth," rather than the "improvement" of employees.

This modern concept of supervision may be defined as follows: Supervision is leadership and the development of leadership within groups which are cooperatively engaged in inspection, research, training, guidance, and evaluation.

THE OLD AND THE NEW SUPERVISION

TRADITIONAL
1. Inspection
2. Focused on the employee
3. Visitation
4. Random and haphazard
5. Imposed and authoritarian
6. One person usually

MODERN
1. Study and analysis
2. Focused on aims, materials, methods, supervisors, employees, environment
3. Demonstrations, intervisitation, workshops, directed reading, bulletins, etc.
4. Definitely organized and planned (scientific)
5. Cooperative and democratic
6. Many persons involved (creative)

THE EIGHT (8) BASIC PRINCIPLES OF THE NEW SUPERVISION

I. Principle of Responsibility
   Authority to act and responsibility for acting must be joined.
   A. If you give responsibility, give authority.
   B. Define employee duties clearly.
   C. Protect employees from criticism by others.
   D. Recognize the rights as well as obligations of employees.
   E. Achieve the aims of a democratic society insofar as it is possible within the area of your work.
   F. Establish a situation favorable to training and learning.
   G. Accept ultimate responsibility for everything done in your section, unit, office, division, department.
   H. Good administration and good supervision are inseparable.

II. Principle of Authority
The success of the supervisor is measured by the extent to which the power of authority is not used.
   A. Exercise simplicity and informality in supervision
   B. Use the simplest machinery of supervision
   C. If it is good for the organization as a whole, it is probably justified.
   D. Seldom be arbitrary or authoritative.
   E. Do not base your work on the power of position or of personality.
   F. Permit and encourage the free expression of opinions.

III. Principle of Self-Growth
The success of the supervisor is measured by the extent to which, and the speed with which, he is no longer needed.
   A. Base criticism on principles, not on specifics.
   B. Point out higher activities to employees.
   C. Train for self-thinking by employees to meet new situations.
   D. Stimulate initiative, self-reliance, and individual responsibility
   E. Concentrate on stimulating the growth of employees rather than on removing defects.

IV. Principle of Individual Worth
Respect for the individual is a paramount consideration in supervision.
   A. Be human and sympathetic in dealing with employees.
   B. Don't nag about things to be done.
   C. Recognize the individual differences among employees and seek opportunities to permit best expression of each personality.

V. Principle of Creative Leadership
The best supervision is that which is not apparent to the employee.
   A. Stimulate, don't drive employees to creative action.
   B. Emphasize doing good things.
   C. Encourage employees to do what they do best.
   D. Do not be too greatly concerned with details of subject or method.
   E. Do not be concerned exclusively with immediate problems and activities.
   F. Reveal higher activities and make them both desired and maximally possible.
   G. Determine procedures in the light of each situation but see that these are derived from a sound basic philosophy.
   H. Aid, inspire, and lead so as to liberate the creative spirit latent in all good employees.

VI. Principle of Success and Failure
There are no unsuccessful employees, only unsuccessful supervisors who have failed to give proper leadership.
   A. Adapt suggestions to the capacities, attitudes, and prejudices of employees.
   B. Be gradual, be progressive, be persistent.
   C. Help the employee find the general principle; have the employee apply his own problem to the general principle.
   D. Give adequate appreciation for good work and honest effort.
   E. Anticipate employee difficulties and help to prevent them.
   F. Encourage employees to do the desirable things they will do anyway.
   G. Judge your supervision by the results it secures.

VII. Principle of Science
Successful supervision is scientific, objective, and experimental. It is based on facts, not on prejudices.
- A. Be cumulative in results.
- B. Never divorce your suggestions from the goals of training.
- C. Don't be impatient of results.
- D. Keep all matters on a professional, not a personal, level.
- E. Do not be concerned exclusively with immediate problems and activities.
- F. Use objective means of determining achievement and rating where possible.

VIII. Principle of Cooperation
Supervision is a cooperative enterprise between supervisor and employee.
- A. Begin with conditions as they are.
- B. Ask opinions of all involved when formulating policies.
- C. Organization is as good as its weakest link.
- D. Let employees help to determine policies and department programs.
- E. Be approachable and accessible—physically and mentally.
- F. Develop pleasant social relationships.

WHAT IS ADMINISTRATION

Administration is concerned with providing the environment, the material facilities, and the operational procedures that will promote the maximum growth and development of supervisors and employees. (Organization is an aspect and a concomitant of administration.)

There is no sharp line of demarcation between supervision and administration; these functions are intimately interrelated and, often, overlapping. They are complementary activities.

I. Practices Commonly Classed as "Supervisory"
- A. Conducting employees' conferences
- B. Visiting sections, units, offices, divisions, departments
- C. Arranging for demonstrations
- D. Examining plans
- E. Suggesting professional reading
- F. Interpreting bulletins
- G. Recommending in-service training courses
- H. Encouraging experimentation
- I. Appraising employee morale
- J. Providing for intervisitation

II. Practices Commonly Classified as "Administrative"
- A. Management of the office
- B. Arrangement of schedules for extra duties
- C. Assignment of rooms or areas
- D. Distribution of supplies
- E. Keeping records and reports
- F. Care of audio-visual materials
- G. Keeping inventory records
- H. Checking record cards and books

I. Programming special activities
  J. Checking on the attendance and punctuality of employees

III. Practices Commonly Classified as Both "Supervisory" and "Administrative"
  A. Program construction
  B. Testing or evaluating outcomes
  C. Personnel accounting
  D. Ordering instructional materials

RESPONSIBILITIES OF THE SUPERVISOR

A person employed in a supervisory capacity must constantly be able to improve his own efficiency and ability. He represent the employer to the employees and only continuous self-examination can make him a capable supervisor.

Leadership and training are the supervisor's responsibility. An efficient working unit is one in which the employees work with the supervisor. It is his job to bring out the best in his employees. He must always be relaxed, courteous, and calm in his association with his employees. Their feelings are important, and a harsh attitude does not develop the most efficient employees.

COMPETENCES OF THE SUPERVISOR

  I. Complete knowledge of the duties and responsibilities of his position.
  II. To be able to organize a job, plan ahead, and carry through.
  III. To have self-confidence and initiative.
  IV. To be able to handle the unexpected situation and make quick decisions.
  V. To be able to properly train subordinates in the positions they are best suited for.
  VI. To be able to keep good human relations among his subordinates.
  VII. To be able to keep good human relations between his subordinates and himself and to earn their respect and trust.

THE PROFESSIONAL SUPERVISOR-EMPLOYEE RELATIONSHIP

There are two kinds of efficiency: one kind is only apparent and is produced in organizations through the exercise of mere discipline; this is but a simulation of the second, or true, efficiency which springs from spontaneous cooperation. If you are a manager, no matter how great or small your responsibility, it is your job, in the final analysis, to create and develop this involuntary cooperation among the people whom you supervise. For, no matter how powerful a combination of money, machines, and materials a company may have, this is a dead and sterile thing without a team of willing, thinking, and articulate people to guide it.

The following 21 points are presented as indicative of the exemplary basic relationship that should exist between supervisor and employee:

1. Each person wants to be liked and respected by his fellow employee and wants to be treated with consideration and respect by his superior.
2. The most competent employee will make an error. However, in a unit where good relations exist between the supervisor and his employees, tenseness and fear do not exist. Thus, errors are not hidden or covered up, and the efficiency of a unit is not impaired.

3. Subordinates resent rules, regulations, or orders that are unreasonable or unexplained.
4. Subordinates are quick to resent unfairness, harshness, injustices, and favoritism.
5. An employee will accept responsibility if he knows that he will be complimented for a job well done, and not too harshly chastised for failure; that his supervisor will check the cause of the failure, and, if it was the supervisor's fault, he will assume the blame therefore. If it was the employee's fault, his supervisor will explain the correct method or means of handling the responsibility.
6. An employee wants to receive credit for a suggestion he has made, that is used. If a suggestion cannot be used, the employee is entitled to an explanation. The supervisor should not say "no" and close the subject.
7. Fear and worry slow up a worker's ability. Poor working environment can impair his physical and mental health. A good supervisor avoids forceful methods, threats, and arguments to get a job done.
8. A forceful supervisor is able to train his employees individually and as a team, and is able to motivate them in the proper channels.
9. A mature supervisor is able to properly evaluate his subordinates and to keep them happy and satisfied.
10. A sensitive supervisor will never patronize his subordinates.
11. A worthy supervisor will respect his employees' confidences.
12. Definite and clear-cut responsibilities should be assigned to each executive.
13. Responsibility should always be coupled with corresponding authority.
14. No change should be made in the scope or responsibilities of a position without a definite understanding to that effect on the part of all persons concerned.
15. No executive or employee, occupying a single position in the organization, should be subject to definite orders from more than one source.
16. Orders should never be given to subordinates over the head of a responsible executive. Rather than do this, the officer in question should be supplanted.
17. Criticisms of subordinates should, whoever possible, be made privately, and in no case should a subordinate be criticized in the presence of executives or employees of equal or lower rank.
18. No dispute or difference between executives or employees as to authority or responsibilities should be considered too trivial for prompt and careful adjudication.
19. Promotions, wage changes, and disciplinary action should always be approved by the executive immediately superior to the one directly responsible.
20. No executive or employee should ever be required, or expected, to be at the same time an assistant to, and critic of, another.
21. Any executive whose work is subject to regular inspection should, wherever practicable, be given the assistance and facilities necessary to enable him to maintain an independent check of the quality of his work.

MINI-TEXT IN SUPERVISION, ADMINISTRATION, MANAGEMENT, AND ORGANIZATION

I. Brief Highlights

Listed concisely and sequentially are major headings and important data in the field for quick recall and review.

A. Levels of Management
Any organization of some size has several levels of management. In terms of a ladder, the levels are:

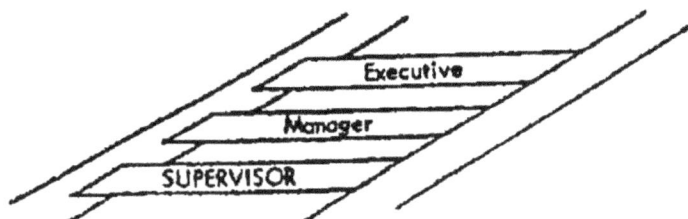

The first level is very important because it is the beginning point of management leadership.

B. What the Supervisor Must Learn
A supervisor must learn to:
1. Deal with people and their differences
2. Get the job done through people
3. Recognize the problems when they exist
4. Overcome obstacles to good performance
5. Evaluate the performance of people
6. Check his own performance in terms of accomplishment

C. A Definition of Supervisor
The term supervisor means any individual having authority, in the interests of the employer, to hire, transfer, suspend, lay-off, recall, promote, discharge, assign, reward, or discipline other employees or responsibility to direct them, or to adjust their grievances, or effectively to recommend such action, if, in connection with the foregoing, exercise of such authority is not of a merely routine or clerical nature but requires the use of independent judgment.

D. Elements of the Team Concept
What is involved in teamwork? The component parts are:
1. Members
2. A leader
3. Goals
4. Plans
5. Cooperation
6. Spirit

E. Principles of Organization
1. A team member must know what his job is.
2. Be sure that the nature and scope of a job are understood.
3. Authority and responsibility should be carefully spelled out.
4. A supervisor should be permitted to make the maximum number of decisions affecting his employees.
5. Employees should report to only one supervisor.
6. A supervisor should direct only as many employees as he can handle effectively.
7. An organization plan should be flexible.

8. Inspection and performance of work should be separate.
9. Organizational problems should receive immediate attention.
10. Assign work in line with ability and experience.

F. The Four Important Parts of Every Job
1. Inherent in every job is the *accountability* for results.
2. A second set of factors in every job is *responsibilities*.
3. Along with duties and responsibilities one must have the *authority* to act within certain limits without obtaining permission to proceed.
4. No job exists in a vacuum. The supervisor is surrounded by key *relationships*.

G. Principles of Delegation
Where work is delegated for the first time, the supervisor should think in terms of these questions:
1. Who is best qualified to do this?
2. Can an employee improve his abilities by doing this?
3. How long should an employee spend on this?
4. Are there any special problems for which he will need guidance?
5. How broad a delegation can I make?

H. Principles of Effective Communications
1. Determine the media.
2. To whom directed?
3. Identification and source authority.
4. Is communication understood?

I. Principles of Work Improvement
1. Most people usually do only the work which is assigned to them.
2. Workers are likely to fit assigned work into the time available to perform it.
3. A good workload usually stimulates output.
4. People usually do their best work when they know that results will be reviewed or inspected.
5. Employees usually feel that someone else is responsible for conditions of work, workplace layout, job methods, type of tools/equipment, and other such factors.
6. Employees are usually defensive about their job security.
7. Employees have natural resistance to change.
8. Employees can support or destroy a supervisor.
9. A supervisor usually earns the respect of his people through his personal example of diligence and efficiency.

J. Areas of Job Improvement
The areas of job improvement are quite numerous, but the most common ones which a supervisor can identify and utilize are:
1. Departmental layout
2. Flow of work
3. Workplace layout
4. Utilization of manpower
5. Work methods
6. Materials handling

7. Utilization
8. Motion economy

K. Seven Key Points in Making Improvements
1. Select the job to be improved
2. Study how it is being done now
3. Question the present method
4. Determine actions to be taken
5. Chart proposed method
6. Get approval and apply
7. Solicit worker participation

l. Corrective Techniques of Job Improvement
Specific Problems
1. Size of workload
2. Inability to meet schedules
3. Strain and fatigue
4. Improper use of men and skills
5. Waste, poor quality, unsafe conditions
6. Bottleneck conditions that hinder output
7. Poor utilization of equipment and machine
8. Efficiency and productivity of labor

General Improvement
1. Departmental layout
2. Flow of work
3. Work plan layout
4. Utilization of manpower
5. Work methods
6. Materials handling
7. Utilization of equipment
8. Motion economy

Corrective Techniques
1. Study with scale model
2. Flow chart study
3. Motion analysis
4. Comparison of units produced to standard allowance
5. Methods analysis
6. Flow chart and equipment study
7. Down time vs. running time
8. Motion analysis

M. A Planning Checklist
1. Objectives
2. Controls
3. Delegations
4. Communications
5. Resources
6. Manpower

7. Equipment
8. Supplies and materials
9. Utilization of time
10. Safety
11. Money
12. Work
13. Timing of improvements

N. Five Characteristics of Good Directions
In order to get results, directions must be:
1. Possible of accomplishment
2. Agreeable with worker interests
3. Related to mission
4. Planned and complete
5. Unmistakably clear

O. Types of Directions
1. Demands or direct orders
2. Requests
3. Suggestion or implication
4. volunteering

P. Controls
A typical listing of the overall areas in which the supervisor should establish controls might be:
1. Manpower
2. Materials
3. Quality of work
4. Quantity of work
5. Time
6. Space
7. Money
8. Methods

Q. Orienting the New Employee
1. Prepare for him
2. Welcome the new employee
3. Orientation for the job
4. Follow-up

R. Checklist for Orienting New Employees   Yes   No
1. Do you appreciate the feelings of new employees when they first report for work?   ___   ___
2. Are you aware of the fact that the new employee must make a big adjustment to his job?   ___   ___
3. Have you given him good reasons for liking the job and the organization?   ___   ___
4. Have you prepared for his first day on the job?   ___   ___
5. Did you welcome him cordially and make him feel needed?   ___   ___

		Yes	No
6.	Did you establish rapport with him so that he feels free to talk and discuss matters with you?	___	___
7.	Did you explain his job to him and his relationship to you?	___	___
8.	Does he know that his work will be evaluated periodically on a basis that is fair and objective?	___	___
9.	Did you introduce him to his fellow workers in such a way that they are likely to accept him?	___	___
10.	Does he know what employee benefits he will receive?	___	___
11.	Does he understand the importance of being on the job and what to do if he must leave his duty station?	___	___
12.	Has he been impressed with the importance of accident prevention and safe practice?	___	___
13.	Does he generally know his way around the department?	___	___
14.	Is he under the guidance of a sponsor who will teach the right way of doing things?	___	___
15.	Do you plan to follow-up so that he will continue to adjust successfully to his job?	___	___

S. Principles of Learning
   1. Motivation
   2. Demonstration or explanation
   3. Practice

T. Causes of Poor Performance
   1. Improper training for job
   2. Wrong tools
   3. Inadequate directions
   4. Lack of supervisory follow-up
   5. Poor communications
   6. Lack of standards of performance
   7. Wrong work habits
   8. Low morale
   9. Other

U. Four Major Steps in On-The-Job Instruction
   1. Prepare the worker
   2. Present the operation
   3. Tryout performance
   4. Follow-up

V. Employees Want Five Things
   1. Security
   2. Opportunity
   3. Recognition
   4. Inclusion
   5. Expression

W. Some Don'ts in Regard to Praise
1. Don't praise a person for something he hasn't done.
2. Don't praise a person unless you can be sincere.
3. Don't be sparing in praise just because your superior withholds it from you.
4. Don't let too much time elapse between good performance and recognition of it

X. How to Gain Your Workers' Confidence
Methods of developing confidence include such things as:
1. Knowing the interests, habits, hobbies of employees
2. Admitting your own inadequacies
3. Sharing and telling of confidence in others
4. Supporting people when they are in trouble
5. Delegating matters that can be well handled
6. Being frank and straightforward about problems and working conditions
7. Encouraging others to bring their problems to you
8. Taking action on problems which impede worker progress

Y. Sources of Employee Problems
On-the-job causes might be such things as:
1. A feeling that favoritism is exercised in assignments
2. Assignment of overtime
3. An undue amount of supervision
4. Changing methods or systems
5. Stealing of ideas or trade secrets
6. Lack of interest in job
7. Threat of reduction in force
8. Ignorance or lack of communications
9. Poor equipment
10. Lack of knowing how supervisor feels toward employee
11. Shift assignments

Off-the-job problems might have to do with:
1. Health
2. Finances
3. Housing
4. Family

Z. The Supervisor's Key to Discipline
There are several key points about discipline which the supervisor should keep in mind:
1. Job discipline is one of the disciplines of life and is directed by the supervisor.
2. It is more important to correct an employee fault than to fix blame for it.
3. Employee performance is affected by problems both on the job and off.
4. Sudden or abrupt changes in behavior can be indications of important employee problems.
5. Problems should be dealt with as soon as possible after they are identified.
6. The attitude of the supervisor may have more to do with solving problems than the techniques of problem solving.
7. Correction of employee behavior should be resorted to only after the supervisor is sure that training or counseling will not be helpful.

8. Be sure to document your disciplinary actions.
9. Make sure that you are disciplining on the basis of facts rather than personal feelings.
10. Take each disciplinary step in order, being careful not to make snap judgments, or decisions based on impatience.

AA. Five Important Processes of Management
1. Planning
2. Organizing
3. Scheduling
4. Controlling
5. Motivating

BB. When the Supervisor Fails to Plan
1. Supervisor creates impression of not knowing his job
2. May lead to excessive overtime
3. Job runs itself—supervisor lacks control
4. Deadlines and appointments missed
5. Parts of the work go undone
6. Work interrupted by emergencies
7. Sets a bad example
8. Uneven workload creates peaks and valleys
9. Too much time on minor details at expense of more important tasks

CC. Fourteen General Principles of Management
1. Division of work
2. Authority and responsibility
3. Discipline
4. Unity of command
5. Unity of direction
6. Subordination of individual interest to general interest
7. Remuneration of personnel
8. Centralization
9. Scalar chain
10. Order
11. Equity
12. Stability of tenure of personnel
13. Initiative
14. Esprit de corps

DD. Change

Bringing about change is perhaps attempted more often, and yet less well understood, than anything else the supervisor does. How do people generally react to change? (People tend to resist change that is imposed upon them by other individuals or circumstances.

Change is characteristic of every situation. It is a part of every real endeavor where the efforts of people are concerned.

1. Why do people resist change?
   People may resist change because of:
   a. Fear of the unknown
   b. Implied criticism
   c. Unpleasant experiences in the past
   d. Fear of loss of status
   e. Threat to the ego
   f. Fear of loss of economic stability

2. How can we best overcome the resistance to change?
   In initiating change, take these steps:
   a. Get ready to sell
   b. Identify sources of help
   c. Anticipate objections
   d. Sell benefits
   e. Listen in depth
   f. Follow up

II. Brief Topical Summaries

   A. Who/What is the Supervisor?
      1. The supervisor is often called the "highest level employee and the lowest level manager."
      2. A supervisor is a member of both management and the work group. He acts as a bridge between the two.
      3. Most problems in supervision are in the area of human relations, or people problems.
      4. Employees expect: Respect, opportunity to learn and to advance, and a sense of belonging, and so forth.
      5. Supervisors are responsible for directing people and organizing work. Planning is of paramount importance.
      6. A position description is a set of duties and responsibilities inherent to a given position.
      7. It is important to keep the position description up-to-date and to provide each employee with his own copy.

   B. The Sociology of Work
      1. People are alike in many ways; however, each individual is unique.
      2. The supervisor is challenged in getting to know employee differences. Acquiring skills in evaluating individuals is an asset.
      3. Maintaining meaningful working relationships in the organization is of great importance.
      4. The supervisor has an obligation to help individuals to develop to their fullest potential.
      5. Job rotation on a planned basis helps to build versatility and to maintain interest and enthusiasm in work groups.
      6. Cross training (job rotation) provides backup skills.

7. The supervisor can help reduce tension by maintaining a sense of humor, providing guidance to employees, and by making reasonable and timely decisions. Employees respond favorably to working under reasonably predictable circumstances.
8. Change is characteristic of all managerial behavior. The supervisor must adjust to changes in procedures, new methods, technological changes, and to a number of new and sometimes challenging situations.
9. To overcome the natural tendency for people to resist change, the supervisor should become more skillful in initiating change.

C. Principles and Practices of Supervision
1. Employees should be required to answer to only one superior.
2. A supervisor can effectively direct only a limited number of employees, depending upon the complexity, variety, and proximity of the jobs involved.
3. The organizational chart presents the organization in graphic form. It reflects lines of authority and responsibility as well as interrelationships of units within the organization.
4. Distribution of work can be improved through an analysis using the "Work Distribution Chart."
5. The "Work Distribution Chart" reflects the division of work within a unit in understandable form.
6. When related tasks are given to an employee, he has a better chance of increasing his skills through training.
7. The individual who is given the responsibility for tasks must also be given the appropriate authority to insure adequate results.
8. The supervisor should delegate repetitive, routine work. Preparation of recurring reports, maintaining leave and attendance records are some examples.
9. Good discipline is essential to good task performance. Discipline is reflected in the actions of employees on the job in the absence of supervision.
10. Disciplinary action may have to be taken when the positive aspects of discipline have failed. Reprimand, warning, and suspension are examples of disciplinary action.
11. If a situation calls for a reprimand, be sure it is deserved and remember it is to be done in private.

D. Dynamic Leadership
1. A style is a personal method or manner of exerting influence.
2. Authoritarian leaders often see themselves as the source of power and authority.
3. The democratic leader often perceives the group as the source of authority and power.
4. Supervisors tend to do better when using the pattern of leadership that is most natural for them.
5. Social scientists suggest that the effective supervisor use the leadership style that best fits the problem or circumstances involved.
6. All four styles—telling, selling, consulting, joining—have their place. Using one does not preclude using the other at another time.

7. The theory X point of view assumes that the average person dislikes work, will avoid it whenever possible, and must be coerced to achieve organizational objectives.
8. The theory Y point of view assumes that the average person considers work to be a natural as play, and, when the individual is committed, he requires little supervision or direction to accomplish desired objectives.
9. The leader's basic assumptions concerning human behavior and human nature affect his actions, decisions, and other managerial practices.
10. Dissatisfaction among employees is often present, but difficult to isolate. The supervisor should seek to weaken dissatisfaction by keeping promises, being sincere and considerate, keeping employees informed, and so forth.
11. Constructive suggestions should be encouraged during the natural progress of the work.

E. Processes for Solving Problems
1. People find their daily tasks more meaningful and satisfying when they can improve them.
2. The causes of problems, or the key factors, are often hidden in the background. Ability to solve problems often involves the ability to isolate them from their backgrounds. There is some substance to the cliché that some persons "can't see the forest for the trees."
3. New procedures are often developed from old ones. Problems should be broken down into manageable parts. New ideas can be adapted from old one.
4. People think differently in problem-solving situations. Using a logical, patterned approach is often useful. One approach found to be useful includes these steps:
   a. Define the problem
   b. Establish objectives
   c. Get the facts
   d. Weigh and decide
   e. Take action
   f. Evaluate action

F. Training for Results
1. Participants respond best when they feel training is important to them.
2. The supervisor has responsibility for the training and development of those who report to him.
3. When training is delegated to others, great care must be exercised to insure the trainer has knowledge, aptitude, and interest for his work as a trainer.
4. Training (learning) of some type goes on continually. The most successful supervisor makes certain the learning contributes in a productive manner to operational goals.
5. New employees are particularly susceptible to training. Older employees facing new job situations require specific training, as well as having need for development and growth opportunities.
6. Training needs require continuous monitoring.
7. The training officer of an agency is a professional with a responsibility to assist supervisors in solving training problems.

8. Many of the self-development steps important to the supervisor's own growth are equally important to the development of peers and subordinates. Knowledge of these is important when the supervisor consults with others on development and growth opportunities.

G. Health, Safety, and Accident Prevention
1. Management-minded supervisors take appropriate measures to assist employees in maintaining health and in assuring safe practices in the work environment.
2. Effective safety training and practices help to avoid injury and accidents.
3. Safety should be a management goal. All infractions of safety which are observed should be corrected without exception.
4. Employees' safety attitude, training and instruction, provision of safe tools and equipment, supervision, and leadership are considered highly important factors which contribute to safety and which can be influenced directly by supervisors.
5. When accidents do occur, they should be investigated promptly for very important reasons, including the fact that information which is gained can be used to prevent accidents in the future.

H. Equal Employment Opportunity
1. The supervisor should endeavor to treat all employees fairly, without regard to religion, race, sex, or national origin.
2. Groups tend to reflect the attitude of the leader. Prejudice can be detected even in very subtle form. Supervisors must strive to create a feeling of mutual respect and confidence in every employee.
3. Complete utilization of all human resources is a national goal. Equitable consideration should be accorded women in the work force, minority-group members, the physically and mentally handicapped, and the older employee. The important question is: "Who can do the job?"
4. Training opportunities, recognition for performance, overtime assignments, promotional opportunities, and all other personnel actions are to be handled on an equitable basis.

I. Improving Communications
1. Communications is achieving understanding between the sender and the receiver of a message. It also means sharing information—the creation of understanding.
2. Communication is basic to all human activity. Words are means of conveying meanings; however, real meanings are in people.
3. There are very practical differences in the effectiveness of one-way, impersonal, and two-way communications. Words spoken face-to-face are better understood. Telephone conversations are effective, but lack the rapport of person-to-person exchanges. The whole person communicates.
4. Cooperation and communication in an organization go hand in hand. When there is a mutual respect between people, spelling out rules and procedures for communicating is unnecessary.
5. There are several barriers to effective communications. These include failure to listen with respect and understanding, lack of skill in feedback, and misinterpreting the meanings of words used by the speaker. It is also common

practice to listen to what we want to hear, and tune out things we do not want to hear.

6. Communication is management's chief problem. The supervisor should accept the challenge to communicate more effectively and to improve interagency and intra-agency communications.
7. The supervisor may often plan for and conduct meetings. The planning phase is critical and may determine the success or the failure of a meeting.
8. Speaking before groups usually requires extra effort. Stage fright may never disappear completely, but it can be controlled.

J. Self-Development
1. Every employee is responsible for his own self-development.
2. Toastmaster and toastmistress clubs offer opportunities to improve skills in oral communications.
3. Planning for one's own self-development is of vital importance. Supervisors know their own strengths and limitations better than anyone else.
4. Many opportunities are open to aid the supervisor in his developmental efforts, including job assignments; training opportunities, both governmental and non-governmental—to include universities and professional conferences and seminars.
5. Programmed instruction offers a means of studying at one's own rate.
6. Where difficulties may arise from a supervisor's being away from his work for training, he may participate in televised home study or correspondence courses to meet his self-development needs.

K. Teaching and Training
1. The Teaching Process
Teaching is encouraging and guiding the learning activities of students toward established goals. In most cases this process consists of five steps: preparation, presentation, summarization, evaluation, and application.

   a. Preparation
   Preparation is two-fold in nature; that of the supervisor and the employee. Preparation by the supervisor is absolutely essential to success. He must know what, when, where, how, and whom he will teach. Some of the factors that should be considered are:
   1) The objectives
   2) The materials needed
   3) The methods to be used
   4) Employee participation
   5) Employee interest
   6) Training aids
   7) Evaluation
   8) Summarization

   Employee preparation consists in preparing the employee to receive the material. Probably the most important single factor in the preparation of the employee is arousing and maintaining his interest. He must know the objectives of the training, why he is there, how the material can be used, and its importance to him.

b. Presentation
In presentation, have a carefully designed plan and follow it. The plan should be accurate and complete, yet flexible enough to meet situations as they arise. The method of presentation will be determined by the particular situation and objectives.

c. Summary
A summary should be made at the end of every training unit and program. In addition, there may be internal summaries depending on the nature of the material being taught. The important thing is that the trainee must always be able to understand how each part of the new material relates to the whole.

d. Application
The supervisor must arrange work so the employee will be given a chance to apply new knowledge or skills while the material is still clear in his mind and interest is high. The trainee does not really know whether he has learned the material until he has been given a chance to apply it. If the material is not applied, it loses most of its value.

e. Evaluation
The purpose of all training is to promote learning. To determine whether the training has been a success or failure, the supervisor must evaluate this learning.
In the broadest sense, evaluation includes all the devices, methods, skills, and techniques used by the supervisor to keep himself and the employees informed as to their progress toward the objectives they are pursuing. The extent to which the employee has mastered the knowledge, skills, and abilities, or changed his attitudes, as determined by the program objectives, is the extent to which instruction has succeeded or failed.
Evaluation should not be confined to the end of the lesson, day, or program but should be used continuously. We shall note later the way this relates to the rest of the teaching process.

2. Teaching Methods
A teaching method is a pattern of identifiable student and instructor activity used in presenting training material.
All supervisors are faced with the problem of deciding which method should be used at a given time.

a. Lecture
The lecture is direct oral presentation of material by the supervisor. The present trend is to place less emphasis on the trainer's activity and more on that of the trainee.

b. Discussion
Teaching by discussion or conference involves using questions and other techniques to arouse interest and focus attention upon certain areas, and by doing so creating a learning situation. This can be one of the most

valuable methods because it gives the employees an opportunity to express their ideas and pool their knowledge.

    c. Demonstration

    The demonstration is used to teach how something works or how to do something. It can be used to show a principle or what the results of a series of actions will be. A well-staged demonstration is particularly effective because it shows proper methods of performance in a realistic manner.

    d. Performance

    Performance is one of the most fundamental of all learning techniques or teaching methods. The trainee may be able to tell how a specific operation should be performed but he cannot be sure he knows how to perform the operation until he has done so.

    As with all methods, there are certain advantages and disadvantages to each method.

    e. Which Method to Use

    Moreover, there are other methods and techniques of teaching. It is difficult to use any method without other methods entering into it. In any learning situation, a combination of methods is usually more effective than any one method alone.

Finally, evaluation must be integrated into the other aspects of the teaching-learning process.

It must be used in the motivation of the trainees; it must be used to assist in developing understanding during the training; and it must be related to employee application of the results of training.

This is distinctly the role of the supervisor.

www.ingramcontent.com/pod-product-compliance
Lightning Source LLC
Chambersburg PA
CBHW081820300426
44116CB00014B/2428